Design Capital 1
The Circuit
Hannah Ellis

Bus-red letters and numbers Tetris into one another. It is summer 2020. 'In light of the Covid-19 pandemic,' a press release that accompanies the Pentagram-designed identity reads, 'we have been looking hard at our options and have consulted with our partners, the broad design community, and the Mayor's office about London Design Festival going ahead in September. The overwhelming consensus is that it should.' (London Design Festival, 2020) Somehow, the identity has managed to escape the restrictions that everyone else is having to live by. Type that has been fast, or outlined, or neon in previous years — never really very different from one year to the next — squashes illegally together. I catch myself (is it... envy?) as the characters move freely on screen, expanding, contracting, cramming themselves together. It's a metaphor for the autumn, say the organisers, when London is going to be 'filled with design'.

It seems unlikely that the city will be filled with much else. Many of the things that had been planned into the year were either cancelled early on or postponed indefinitely. Design events too, an unsuspecting casualty of the pandemic. Around the world, a packed calendar of similar festivals, biennials, and weeks has been cleared by uncertainty. London Design Festival is unwaveringly optimistic, though. Established in 2003 by Ben Evans and Jon Sorrell, also co-founders of London Design Biennial,[1] the seventeenth outing of the Festival will also be the first major event to take place across Europe. Fewer international visitors are anticipated (for obvious reasons) but this has reframed this year's intent. Instead of a sprawling collection of exhibitions, London Design Festival 2020 will be smaller in scale, a mixture of real life exhibits and online content. It is billed as 'a Festival for Londoners with a strong focus on the local. ' (2020)

I had only just moved out of London. Not just out of but *away* from the capital, back to a city that does not have to worry about festivals or biennials, or design events at all, because it does not suffer to the same extent with weighty traditions of 'culture' and — perhaps partly because of that — isn't a place people tend to want to visit. Caught straddling that both-space of a recent life change, I was still trying to negotiate what 'local' means in practice. Physically, I was 'local' in my hometown. But I was still socially and vocationally 'local' elsewhere, an adoptee of London, digitally commuting and still tuning into the city's concerns. Between reading press releases and statements from the Festival, I watch the national news reporting of daily death tolls and hospital admissions. Video clips show tube carriages and red buses still busy with people (squashed illegally, too) despite the advice to stay and work at home. About two weeks after the Festival is confirmed to be going ahead, another statement is issued, this time by the Mayor's office. Forty-four Transport for London workers — mainly bus drivers who, unlike designers, were unable to work on a MacBook or from home — are reported to have died from Covid. (Mayor of London, 2020) The statistic prods around the city's inequalities. Forty-four people who were Londoners, too. As the months pass, this number rises, disproportionately weighted against BIPOC. When the press covers this imbalanced statistic, they talk briefly about structural inequities, and say that the drivers were put in positions of unnecessary risk: by TfL, who failed to adequately protect their staff; by the people who travelled gratuitously; worst, by the minority who screamed and spat and coughed as people tried to do and keep their jobs. Questions are raised (and never really answered) about who an essential worker is and what qualifies their work as 'essential'. Also about the responsibilities of employers and contractors to their staff, the public's responsibilities to one another.

London Design Festival, though, is silent. There is no mention of the city or its residents in the statements or interviews with co-founders that happen in the following weeks. 'Local', I try to remember, is not an easy thing to contemplate across nine and a half million residents. Even though it suggests a level of active participation with or concern for the area and people, the self-declared 'Festival for Londoners' is determined not to be drawn into these discussions. Design events are about design, the silence says. They are not about bus drivers, or Whiteness, the unbearable density of the city or infection rates that threaten to spike after gathering. These things are outside of the discipline, the silence confirms.

Are they though? Should they be? Truthfully, I never completely manage to get my head around the push to organise an event at a time of genuine life and death. Travel restrictions and cancelled plans have created a vacuum, says the press release, which has left designers across and beyond the city 'hungry for content.' (London Design Festival, 2020) The Festival doesn't explicitly mention that it has more than the one 'local' focus: it cuts across communities — London, of course, but also design. And perhaps because I was navigating my own understanding of multiple 'locals' at the same time, mentally between the place I knew well and the place that I assumed I knew, a place that had changed in the decade I had been gone into something I barely recognised, this realisation felt more acute. The place I thought I had rights to — the hometown that I had been born in, grown in, that taught me to drop Ts as I spoke — was a place I was no longer tethered to.

As I try to reorientate myself, I think about this point a lot: the places we claim to be locals, and the places (not always geographic) we really are. Also about bored designers who seem to outweigh the London public. Unable, in this moment of extremity, to tie itself meaningfully into the immediate place and people, the Festival reveals an organisational mindset that is perhaps less obvious in other years. It exposes how it does or doesn't consider how it acts beyond itself, or what it sustains by putting design above all else. 'It is important that major events like the Festival happen this autumn,' says the press release, 'not least as a symbol of London's determination to maintain its creative and cultural leadership.' Which London? Whose London? What is important, really, is not the place or the people, but leadership by design. Separating into parts is a habitual practice, and shows up not just in London but across Europe and in other Western design events that want to lead, too. But separating into parts also avoids thinking about design events as a whole, that could be and are about bus drivers, and Whiteness, and the unbearable density of the city, and infection rates that threaten to spike after gathering — just as much as they are about design.

> 'It's worth reminding ourselves,' Ben Evans says mid-way through an interview that happens on Zoom a few weeks after the first announcement, 'that in the design sector when we started in 2003, I think there were five or six global cities doing promotional design events. At last count, there were well over 150 global cities doing it.' (Exposure London, 2020)

Through scale and longevity, London Design Festival has played more than a small part in defining the shape and terms of nearby design events. In a 2012 review, design curator Justine Boussard describes the event as having 'become a potent force in defining and directing contemporary design.' (Boussard, 2013, p. 411) An institution created by repetition, for ten days each year, the organisers become "master-curators," or — as Boussard calls them — the 'sole arbiters of good design.' (p. 410) What results is a top down articulation of what is considered good or important in design at any one moment. A reflexive kind of attention follows the events, so that tradition quickly establishes itself; highlights repeat on the design blogs, written up into overenthusiastic 'Top Ten Things to See at...' and 'Our Five Favourite Picks...' lists that recommend readers towards the things that are 'not to be missed' and away from the others. Each year is anticipated and covered because it was the year before. Pandemic or otherwise, what is important to the event is continuing. And, for continuity's sake, it is not really in the event's best interests to look too closely at the fundamentals that have been taken for granted in the process.

Caught on figures of growth, I almost don't notice the 'promotional' which slips into the conversation. In the seventeen years since it first began, London Design Festival and others like it have cultivated strict routines of advocacy across towns and cities, restructuring them entirely in the name of design. Every year or two, for a week, a month, or more, thousands of visitors (more, often, than the city holds in residence) fly in and out to see the shows on typography, or graphic design, or products and architecture that fill up galleries and empty spaces. Promoting the host city as much as design itself, agendas and stakeholders knot themselves around the events. Budgets of public and private money keep the pace; I never manage to completely get my head around the numbers. Councils and governments set aside hundreds of thousands — sometimes millions, depending on where you are — of pounds to produce temporary installations and exhibitions. (My designer friends visit and take photos; it is the sort of work, though, that my non-designer friends shrug at, dispassionately.)

'Well, to be absolutely honest,' John Sorrell picks up and carries on Evans' thought, 'and I'm not in any way being uncomplimentary to them, but *most* of them have copied what we've done. And it's very nice to be able to say that.' Most of the remaining conversation follows the party line that good design is good for business. 'Because the more cities in the world that embrace design and recognise how important it is to their society and to their economies, the better the world will be.' (Exposure London, 2020) Design's proposed economic benefit is about as close to a mention of any kind of essentialness as Evans and Sorrell come. It's a strained suggestion, full of assumed and vaporous positives that dissipate as soon as you try to get close to them. (What constitutes 'design', and what about the work that cannot be showcased? How exactly does economic benefit translate into a better world? What is 'better' anyway — and for whom?) Dubious connections do not prevent the Festival being discussed as some kind of antidote to threats of recession, though. 'Before Covid, [the "creative industry"] was delivering £111.7 billion a year to the UK economy, and providing well over two million jobs,' says Sorrell. 'If you think about the size of it, it's bigger than the life sciences, and the oil and gas industries combined. So it's an absolutely enormous and very important sector.' (2020) They are the kind of figures that are too large to fully know what to do with, but ones that sound important as government debts increase. 'And, by the way,' he continues, 'it's also growing at more than five times the rate of the UK economy as a whole.' (Whether that remains true when the economy folds in on itself isn't elaborated on.) Employment, much like in other industries, is an immediate concern. This year the Festival programme will also include a Freelancer Portal because small studios and the self-employed have felt a specific kind of misery during the pandemic.[2] It is important to support one another at a time like this, Evans and Sorrell say.

I wait for one of them to dissect the politics that link periods of sickness — yours, individually, or at societal-scale — axiomatically to destitution, or ask why an industry set on 'problem solving' didn't predict that the precarious model of employment it relied on might be a problem in itself. To question which people and bodies this structure excludes. For a moment I believe that they might, then realise they won't; having seen the Festival up close, I wasn't sure how I'd let my expectations get so high. By my own admission, I am not usually a person who enjoys these sorts of events, or the design they revere. In September 2016, I stumbled — quite literally and by accident — into London Design Festival. The installation that I had come across on my way to somewhere else was one of Asif Khan's *Forests*: three transparent pavilions filled with plants, produced in collaboration with MINI Living, a long-term research project of MINI BMW. *Forests*, I read, had been designed with the idea of providing 'moments of calm' in the city, reimagining what relaxation might look like. The pavilions had been placed near to Old Street station, an area also known to some as Silicon Roundabout, bloated by creative-tech money. (Box has an office nearby, Adobe does too.) I had fallen into 'Connect': plants were accompanied by moveable benches and, with a little pushing and rearranging, the space could be transformed from a meditative seating area into a site for 'co-working jams.'

Forests featured heavily on design blogs as one of those things that was 'not to be missed.' It photographed well — it was beautiful, the light through corrugated polycarbonate, falling on Alocasia and Philodendron leaves — an aesthetic tailored towards attention and algorithms, and so it appeared all over Instagram, too. But it was also the kind of design that makes claims far beyond what it's capable of. The communities around the area don't mix, the caption read. I wasn't sure if I was meant to be surprised that the office workers, the residential mixture of students, new renters and long-term occupants (who had seen the area go from working-class neighbourhood to a Disneyland of storage container coffee shops, expensive restaurants, and creative shops and workspaces), and the tourists who passed through as part of their stay — everyone living on different timescales and economic planes — didn't have places in their lives for one another. Outside of the polycarbonate box, traffic heaved and sirens raced down and around City Road on their way to an emergency. This plant-filled corridor, I read further, was a place where that mixing could happen, an oasis in the middle of the capital.

The caption didn't specify how, exactly, these communities would mix, or why they might want to in the first place. I was confused by this at the time, and again, years later, when I looked the project up. Mixing is one of those things presumed to have value in and of itself, presented as easy and utopian. Strangers would sit together inside this urban greenhouse, and their lives would diffuse into one another. But whether any of those groups would — or wanted to — and what that would mean as individuals bought lives informed by things like class, and race and ethnicity, and gender was presented as an irrelevance. As Evans and Sorrell talk about employment, never quite getting to whether precarity might be stacked against disabled people, mothers, poor people, I remember Arturo Escobar's opening questions in *Designs for the Pluriverse* (2018). The first chapter, 'Design for the Real World', borrows its name from Victor Papanek's 1971 book, which often rereads as being as relevant as when it was when first published:

'But which "World"?', Escobar asks.

'What "Design"? What "Real"?' (Escobar, 2018, p. 23)

I wasn't aware of it at the time, but *Forests*, and later, London Design Festival as a whole, as I kept track of it in the years afterwards, or passed through it, or saw it everywhere on social media, became a kind of personal metaphor for the conflicts and frustrations I was having. Outside of the container I was a resident, financially struggling in (and perhaps against) a city that is famous for making life unliveable. I was a practitioner, too, frustrated as the subject — to my mind — continually missed the point and yet still managed to aggrandise *d*esign into *D*esign: a subject of experts. I couldn't locate myself in the Festival's celebration of either 'London' or 'Design.' I laughed as I read that MINI Living were researching urban mobility, remembering how intensely I had felt giving mine up, forced to make a choice between independent travel and shelter, selling the car that gave me an escape from the city to make rent.

   Whether we realise it or not, our worldview leaves a trace on what we create, writes Escobar, and these traces can be read by others. What 'Real' and 'World' meant to me — as a resident, but as a designer, too — was patently not important to the 'potent force' driving and defining design from a London centre. I could tell. But I also knew that, even accidentally, I had become one of hundreds of thousands of people who were head-counted, supporting this definition further. My body's presence was someone else's measurement of success. There are no metrics to record or describe broader frustrations and conflicts and no place for them, anyway, within an event that is really about 'promotion.'

A logic-driven silence says a 'design event' is obviously and exclusively about design. But a more necessarily complex conclusion of what they do or are or how they exist in the world is slightly harder to pin down. They are slippery things, tricky to articulate precisely because of the fundamentals we take for granted, and subject to unofficial precursors — like 'promotional' — that change their meaning entirely.

'Events' is too big a category to file under, a cluttering of festivals and weeks and biennials, piling together the exhibitions that take over a city for days, weeks, sometimes months. Flags are planted overnight and lay claim to a place that has been conquered by design. From the outside, beyond the length of time that they stretch out and over a city for, they behave largely in the same way, or at least appear to. Differentiation requires a bit of etymological digging: take, for example, the meaning of 'festival' — a day or period of celebration, usually religious. For the most part, design festivals are annual, celebrating the subject with Gregorian predictability, much like the dedicated Weeks that block out one fifty-second of the industry calendar. Language puts 'design' next to deities and, traced back far enough, 'festival' can be followed through iterations of Old French and Latin — *festivalis, festivus* — to the root of *festa*, for feast. A day of dedication or a celebratory meal; in this case, what is gorged upon is not good food and wine, but an overabundance of D/design. (They should not, I realise later on, be confused as moments for close examination or interrogation; further backwards still, *festa* is one step removed from *festus* — joyous.)

Design biennials (*biennales*, if you're committed to the Italian) are more complicated still. As both an adjective and a noun, 'biennial' starts with botany: a plant with a lifecycle — from seed, through growth and flowering, to eventual expiration — of two years. First used in Ancient Greece to determine two-yearly plants from those that were one-yearly or others that seemed to regenerate forever, it was not until the 17th century that the word was used to mean anything that occurred one year, and skipped the next. It was much later, in the mid-1900s, after Venice, that it was used to define syncopated events: usually a large scale art exhibition presented for and towards an international audience.

Design enters somewhere in between these two dates, as the lineage of festivals and biennials and other similar events overlap. Mid-way through the Industrial Revolution, early design events that shared the international ambitions of contemporary biennials — expositions (*exponere:* expose, publish, explain) and world fairs (Middle English: a periodic gathering for the sale of goods, later an exhibition to promote particular products)[3] — emerged as countries competed to be seen. By this time, ideas of joyous dedication or celebration at smaller scales had already been replaced by competitive largeness. Promotion was central to these early events. In 1844, the *Exposition des Produits de l'Industrie Française,* widely thought of as the first international 'design event', had gained a reputation for bringing together feats of manufacturing that escaped France's country borders. For half a century, the event had increased in size, starting as a protectionist attempt to shield French manufacturers from economic damage caused by cheaper English products. Early versions of the Exposition had been small, and stalls were set out with French-made products for visitors to buy. Browsing, it turned out, was more popular though — both with the general public and with makers themselves — a realisation that was quickly picked up on by officials and turned into strategy. In 1834, the President of the Societé Royale d'Emulation, Jacques Boucher de Perthes, spoke of the benefits that came out of peer-assessment, saying: 'It is here that the producer brings the fruit of his labour side by side with that of his neighbour — takes the measure of his efforts, estimates the merits of his productions ... exhibitions are better than prohibitions, which tend to separate men and isolate them.' (Greenhalgh, 1988, p. 10) French makers, so the theory went, would be encouraged to continue to improve their work, cycling between display, constructive nosiness, and a desire for self-betterment.

It was through repetition, though, the two or more yearly cycles of growth and improvement, that the promotional value outgrew that of design itself. By its tenth iteration in 1844, the Exposition, publishing outwards, had become something else entirely — both in intent and scale. Catalogues that documented previous events had caught attentions across Europe. Stalls were replaced by a temporary building on the Champs-Élysées that was purpose-built for the two month exhibition. Almost 4,000 items were on display: from Fine and Decorative Arts, to 'machines to drill the ground for water, to transform sea-water into fresh water, to heat rooms, and improved devices for electroplating with gold or silver.' (Burat, cited in Daniels, 2013, p. 5) For a while, Paris was the centre-point crossing of industrial production and pageantry. As a city, it could command attention. It was seen to be capable of changing the world.

Happening at a time of imperial power struggles, the Exposition quickly inspired competitors. Britain, never to appear outdone, held the Great Exhibition shortly afterwards in 1851, in the purpose-built Crystal Palace. Without precedents to refer back to, early events had to 'invent a way of showing manufactured objects so as to render them meaningful beyond themselves.' (Greenhalgh, 1988, p. 3) Entertainment, spectacle and pageantry became integral elements of display. The size of a small city itself, covering nineteen acres of ground, the Crystal Palace was built over and around the mature trees of Hyde Park that stood in its way.

(Later, I read that the displays inside were ten miles long, and ache at the thought.) Overseen by Prince Albert, thirty-four nations, some 15,000 individual exhibitors, took part in the one-off event.

Architecture was used metaphorically. If the Paris expositions had advocated for industrially-driven progress, the Great Exhibition stood for bigness and dominion. As much as anything else, the Exhibition acted as a show of importing ability. Writing in *Ephemeral Vistas,* historian and curator Paul Greenhalgh notes that 'despite a quasi-educational slant, the overall attitude and feeling was one of stocktaking, of an accountant's inventory of a company's possessions.' (1988, p. 54) Of the thousands of objects on show to the public, half were examples of products of Britain and the countries that it had forced into subjugation.[4] On display were raw materials, commodities, fine art pieces, and manufacturing processes: printing presses that worked and demystified production to a public audience; the 105.6 carats of the Koh-i-Noor diamond; tapestries and textiles; steam-powered trains; cotton was refined and spun and woven in front of visitors' eyes. Empire, he continues, was seen as 'a commodity, a thing more important than but not dissimilar to shawls, ironwork, flax, or indeed, sculpture... This point was reinforced by the way the countries within the empire were exhibited, as quantifiable batches of produce rather than as cultures.'

Whilst histories and cultures that had been interrupted, flattened, or erased entirely by colonisation were objectified and reduced into one inside the Crystal Palace, the imbalance of power would see the inverse happen across Europe. Countries were opened up. Railways had cut lines across the continent; new cartographies formed around them. Many people would later point to the Exhibition, converging as it did with a quickly democratising and cheapening transport infrastructure, as the beginning of cultural tourism on a massive scale. Over the course of five-and-a-half months, six million people visited The Exhibition — because they could. A requirement of the event was that it would be self-financing, and entry to visitors was ticketed. It broke even, and then some. In total, the Exhibition made a profit of £186,000 (which, adjusted for inflation, works out at somewhere between £18–26 million today) (Picard, 2009) and the surplus was folded back into the surrounding area, funding London's museum district, the straight line stretch from South Kensington tube station to Hyde Park colloquially known as Albertopolis. The Great Exhibition, in its success, was soon followed by others as nations were enticed by a heady mix of uncritical attention and easy money: the Exhibition of the Industry of All Nations (New York, 1853–4); the Exposition Universelle (Paris, 1855); the Ottoman General Exposition (Istanbul, 1863). Within twenty years, world fairs had established themselves as a mode of display of the powerful, and repeated their idea of 'progress' around the world.

These early events are important, not because they are necessarily brilliant, or noteworthy in critical ways, but because of the precedent they set. Industry and empire were inextricably linked. Early displays of 'progress' shaped what would come: immediately afterwards; later; today; tomorrow. The Expositions and Exhibitions imagined by European countries during the fervour of the Scientific and Industrial Revolution happily uncoupled design from the contexts around it. Form and function — neither mattered more than the other because both were irrelevant — design objects, when collected together into an event, were a political tool. As a discipline, design became symbolic of being a key player in the world economy, of having power, real or imagined, where others had none.

This ancestry is what Escobar calls the 'active historical reality' that contemporary design has to confront: a foundational way of being that informs the design, and design events, today. Design is ontological, he writes. Decisions made around material things and immaterial infrastructures inscribe themselves into the way we understand, and continue to understand, the world. (Anne-Marie Willis describes this process as one where we design and, in doing so, 'we are designed by our designing and by that which we have designed'.) (2006) No matter how conceptually far away, contemporary events always derive from these predecessors. For any meaningful 'reorientation of design' towards the future to happen, writes Escobar, it's important to understand this past-present entanglement:

> Recognising those historical aspects of our historicity that seem buried in a long-gone past — which requires paying attention to the realm of myth and story in shaping our worlds — is part and parcel of design's coming to terms with the very historicity of the worlds and things in the current tumultuous age.[5] (Escobar, 2018, p. 15)

And so these early events, the Great Exhibition et al., are important because in their magnitude they celebrate the moment where the world was fractured by Western modernity. Euro-centred design events were born out of a churning mixture of colonisation, diffuse power relations, and early globalisation. Design (like nearby disciplines of art and architecture) was now something that had power beyond and outside of itself. The possibility of what design could do lay beyond actual utility; instead, value lay in what a collection of artefacts implied — specific notions of learning, manufacturing skill, access to resources, material wealth —

and the extent to which these could be weaponised against others. Escobar writes:

> The power of tools and design to shape being and identity is eloquently attested by the buzz caused by the world's fairs, from the mid-nineteenth century till today, which became showcases for designs embodying the technological and cultural accomplishments of the age. The famous Crystal Palace Exhibition in London in 1851 paraded for the first time in a specially designed space the technologies, trinkets, and prototypes of the day — power looms, pumps, steam engines, industrial machines. As visitors made their way through the glass cathedral, it became clear to them that not all peoples in the world had achieved the same level of "development," for there was no way the arts from "the stationary East" nor the handicrafts from "the aborigines" could ever match the "progress" of the West. Machines, after all, were "the measure of men". (Escobar, 2018, p. 31)

World fairs, he continues, were 'shrines for the collective adoration of the "civilisation" and progress brought about by the Enlightenment era.' Events similar to the early fairs of Paris had happened across the world since the Middle Ages. For hundreds of years, merchants travelled and sold commodity goods across Asia, along the Silk Road, or following the sophisticated networks between Western African nations and the Kingdom of Benin. But the scale and loudness of modern World Fairs and Exhibitions would define new terms of engagement. Design and its objects symbolic of 'progress' were now an integral part of modern society. Medals of excellence, written up for posterity into gold and cloth-bound volumes offered definitive answers to questions of 'World' and 'Design' and 'Real', cannibalising non-Western histories in the process. The very systems that created the disparate wealth needed for the Industrial Revolution to take place — coloniality, empire — were dismissed as unrelated happenstance.

Because of their enduring popularity, these Expositions and Exhibitions did not have to wrestle with their own authenticity or unpick the cause and effect of seeing and being seen: the continued power dynamics of early attention economies, the choice of who and what and how to present, or why, and the impacts that these decisions had. From their mid-nineteenth century beginnings, European expositions proliferate — then specialise and repeat. In 1895, the arts separate off from manufacturing in Venice, Italy, with the first 'biennial' proper, a multi-exhibition spectacle in art. Established to celebrate King Umberto I and Margherita of Savoy's silver wedding anniversary, it would commemorate the occasion every other year until the present day. Architecture begins to peel away from 1933 with La Triennale di Milano, as the concerns of the disciplines began to diverge. But Venice would remain one of a kind for almost six decades. The so-called second wave of biennials crested between 1950 and 1980, focussing on redefinition: 'regionalism and attempt[ing] to bring the local artistic endeavours to international attention to redefine cultural networks across geopolitical divides.' (Komorowski, 2018, p. 1) Venice served as a major inspiration for the first São Paulo Biennial in 1951, and was quickly followed by others. In 1955, both the Egyptian Biennale de la Mediterrané (Alexandria) and The Biennial of Graphic Arts, Ljubljana, Slovenia (formerly Yugoslavia) were established, fuelled, according to researcher and academic Wiktor Komorowski, by 'the search for a soft power strategy that could place a peripheral country on the map of international relations.' (Komorowski, 2018, p. 6) Motivated by the experience of 'cultural isolation', the latter began with aims not dissimilar to Paris' Exposition — as a national competition for printmakers, allowing them to link to practitioners outside of the Soviet Union and 'help them to make their mark on the emerging global art map.' (Komorowski, 2018, p. 6)

Ljubljana would be joined shortly afterwards, in 1963, by the Brno International Biennial of Graphic Design, as designers created a platform for critical outrage at the Cold War. Despite a celebratory origin, biennials would continue to follow these politicised agendas, and increasingly emerge as counters to Western ways of thinking. The First Biennale of Arab Art, Baghdad (Iraq, 1974) — a nomadic biennial — hoped to use the format of an art biennial to foreground a region 'united by a shared heritage and recent colonial past, and collectively facing comparable contemporary challenges.' (Alsaden, 2019, p. 124) The Havana Biennial, similarly, came out of 'the idea to create a platform for national and international recognition for Caribbean and Latin American artists' in 1986. (Delgado, 2018) Dak'Art was formed in 1990 to establish an art market within Senegal, and 'promote the latest examples of contemporary art in Africa' (Nzewi, 2013, p. 1) — thirty years after Senegal's independence from France — continuing the energy and ambitions of the first World Festival of Black Arts, held in Dakar in 1966, into a regular and repeating event. Where Venice had celebrated royal matrimony, much later biennials would also be used to remember the brutality of politics and the state. The Gwangju Biennale was founded in 1995, commemorating lives lost during the pro-democracy protest of the Gwangju Uprising five years earlier. In 2005, the Riwaq Biennale was established to protect and promote the heritage of Palestine, 'recognising the challenging complexities of preserving Palestinian collective memory.' (Bshara, 2017, p. 76) It is not a complete timeline by any means; there are so many biennials that I lose track of them repeatedly. But throughout all disciplines — art, architecture, but also design — there is a clear splitting off that happens to biennials and biennial-ish events. Two categories emerge: those that understood, inherently, the ontology of these events, the discipline, and the power structures that surrounded them; and those that didn't. The first rooted themselves in social, cultural, and political circumstances. The latter, the Western European and American events, modern in both birth and attitude, never had (or chose) to think too deeply about their own existence. They had, or so history confirmed to them, defined the form.

Biennials, though, are an exception in the too-large category of 'events' that happen in and around design. Where biennials (in art and architecture especially) have been subject to critical examination, research and theory, design events like festivals and weeks managed, once established, to continue largely outside of the realms of scrutiny. Design and its showcasing — the kind that emerged out of Britain and North America in the years that followed World War II — had an entirely different motive. It was not about collective remembering, or protest, or understanding the complexity of global relationships. Value, for the West, continued to lie in what design implied.

Exactly a century after the Great Exhibition, the Festival of Britain, held in 1951, was hoped to be a 'tonic to the nation', through a series of exhibitions that commemorated British "values" and manufacturing. Staggering with debt, a celebration through design was intended to revitalise post-war Britain and the remnants of Empire — now rebranded as the communal-sounding 'Commonwealth.' Land was dragged from the River Thames, and craters left by wartime explosions were filled in. The newly reclaimed land was called the Southbank and, departing from classical aesthetics, pavilions that signified space-age futurism were built on top. But in between celebrations and exhibitions the intention was to quietly use modernism to reactivate ideas of empire. Abram Games' celebrated Britannia sat right at the centre: a war-helmeted woman, sharpened by compass points and softened by bunting. The logo hides colonialism neatly away, writes Jo Littler in *Festering Britain* (2006, p. 25), 'as imperialism is divested of some of its heavy grandiose swagger and portrayed instead through clean modern lines.' Between adverts for domestic items and paintings of newly built power stations, I find the sentiment (less subtly) written into the Festival catalog. 'Taken together, [the exhibitions] will add up to one united act of national reassessment, and one corporate reaffirmation of faith in the nation's future.' (The Festival of Britain, 1951, p. 6)

Britain's fragile outward appearances, boosted by modernist design, aligned more obviously with the corporate branding strategies and advertising that had begun to define the era in the West, than the biennials that would begin to emerge elsewhere. In North America, design events showcased 'American Dream' type values at home and abroad. Eisenhower's cabinet, however, utilised design in much more aggressive ways to influence national image. In the same way that the CIA used the Abstract Expressionism of Jackson Pollock and Mark Rothko only a few years before, a shadow account of funding was allocated for touring trade shows and exhibitions to improve the USA's image abroad. Concealing the organisation role of the Government, 'psychological warfare' was waged through a careful selection of commercial partners, curated into shows that intruded into Eastern Europe, Asia, and Africa. By 1963, around 300 of these exhibitions had happened across the world, admitting millions of visitors. Curated entirely by the USA government, design was reduced to a stagecraft object of ventriloquism. Lucius D Battle, then the Assistant Secretary of State, said: 'American "things" — packages and products — make a terrific impact on people so far as image-building is concerned.' (Castillo, 2017, p. 49) Compared to film, and art, design felt trustworthy. It hid through utility, a veneer of presumed neutrality and claimed universality, the ideologies that other arts willingly pushed to the surface.

From the mid-century onwards, the distinction between festivals and weeks and biennials becomes vague. Events slip from one form to another. Exhibitions become regular and cyclical. Festivals get bigger, their size tiring them out until they repeat more slowly, biennially, rather than annually. The design weeks that spread from capitals to the provinces begin to stretch out, expanding for visitors and beyond a definable fraction of a year. Some biennials happen once and then never again. Or, they speed up, forgoing the rest period between years to become 'festivals' that describe themselves in exactly the same way as they had done before. Writing in *Archis Volume 54: On Biennials,* curator Brendan Cormier gives up on definition, noting that '[t]here is only one rule for a biennial: that it happens every two years.' (Cormier, 2018, p. 7) Without any clear guide, the events become things that people don't know quite what to do with. There is nothing that can be categorically pinned to say: a festival is *this,* a biennial is *that.*[6] Some events become broad overviews of the subject. Others specialise down into niches. Many occupy a noncommittal space somewhere between the two.

One thing that is certain, though: that there are *lots.* The proliferation of events in all forms since the mid-twentieth century leaves us (according to many) at a point of fatigue, as events layer up over cities and make them heavy. An estimate in 2016, adding up the number of printed programmes that save places for biennials on library shelves, put the number at somewhere over a hundred. (Grandal Montero, 2012) Two years later, another survey across disciplines placed the number of 'biennials' — the pair of quotation marks including annual events, as well as those that are two- and three-yearly — around the world at 316, (Kolb & Patel, 2018, p. 15) higher even than Evans' and Sorrell's design-only estimate. But without structure to refer back to, design events have become more of a question of quantity rather than quality. Size matters. Amount matters. For a place to be seen as an important contributor, it must have leapfrogging or sprawling events, metronomically keeping design in a city-wide rhythm. Curators and organisers and exhibiting designers are interviewed about their ambitions and intents, so that the leapfrogging or sprawling events keep time in online space, too.

Reading about similar events in other disciplines, or watching the interviews, I struggle with the way that discourse happens at a distance. At no point in the discussions of intent, in between the tick-tocking beats of online promotion, am I asked to consider the attendee. A person who witnesses the event — not in its ideal form — but partially and behind the heads of others. Or hurriedly on a lunch break. With children (and low boredom thresholds) in tow. As a nuisance in their home town.

In *Seven Years* (2019), art critic Maria Lind writes about the bodily and emotional toll that is part of attending these exhibition-events: the summer heat and the queuing, the sweating, the aching and tired legs. Reflecting back on Alejandro Cesarco's *Methodology*, she writes: 'Experiencing this short but touching video was worth all my frustration and disappointment with the 2011 Venice Biennale.' (p. 37) Her contention, she continues, is with 'Teflon biennials.' After proliferating wildly, events smoothed themselves down in trying to appeal to everyone, anyone, becoming frictionless as a result. There are no jagged moments that snag, or catch, or unravel you completely. For Lind, these contemporary events occupy the same kind of capitalist Junkspace that Rem Koolhaas writes about — polished, consumer-friendly spaces, something to move through rather than think too much about:

> They operate in roughly the same way as a smoothly crafted shopping mall which wants to create a seemingly effortless experience so as to make you feel good. At the Teflon Biennial very little, or nothing, stands out. [...] Instead, visitors are flushed through a well-designed and aptly engineered biennale where these is just enough stimulation to avoid boredom and keep you prepared to consume more. (Lind, 2019, p. 37)

It is October 2019. I am not sure if I feel flushed, exactly, per Lind. In fact, the feeling I have is more one of being shoved and elbowed. I am in Eindhoven for Dutch Design Week — along with thousands of others. *If not now, then when?* repeats and glitches across the city in cyber green and black and white. *If not now, now, now* — it's difficult to ignore, as posters animate and glitch in the street like screens exposing their code — *then when? when? when?* — artificial RGB green standing out from everything around it. (Mirko Borsche's neon yellow identity for the Venice Pavilion in 2019 visually 'contaminated' the city in similar ways.) Flags, the kind that you don't notice until their advertising changes, make lazy arches into the street and tap-tap-tap in the wind against their poles. The brand is driven through Eindhoven on the side of Renault-sponsored cars that take people from one site to another; floats just beneath the surface of the canals

on the cover of guide-maps that have drowned. Some lucky
ones have been rescued. Lying by the canal-side they papier-
mâché themselves into the pavement.

As the identity fuses itself into the environment around
it, I try to figure out who, or what, is being interrogated,
and to what end. *If not now, then when?* is the kind of urgent
question designers love: simple but grandiose. Also: vague
and entirely unanswerable. One eroteme away from 'it's
now or never', it's the type of solution-focused question that
makes me panic. It demands immediacy, an ability to think
and react deliberately and with unwavering confidence on
the spot — skills I do not possess. It follows on from the
previous year's provocation: *if not us, then who?* I assume
(I never find out for certain) that 'us' means designers, most
likely of the capital-D kind of Design.

Together, the questions nod to change-making,
sustainability perhaps, but Dutch Design Week stops short
of a specific meaning, which is difficult to wrap your head
around at such scale. According to the website, it is 'the
biggest design event in Northern Europe', and in excess of
350,000 visitors come to see the work of more than 2,600
designers. (The resident population of Eindhoven itself
is only slightly more at 359,000.) There are 143 separate
locations across nine distinct regions of the city and its
semi-industrial suburbs. To the south-east, Campina, a
repurposed milk factory, is used for main Educational
Partner Design Academy Eindhoven's end-of-year show,
hosting 181 graduating students. To the north-west — just
past PSV Eindhoven's home ground, the Philips Stadium
— the company's former factories and power plant host
maker-space exhibitions. Dutch Design Week is sprawling
and large to the extent that walking from one peripheral site
to another leaves your body aching for deep sleep and your
legs restless. There is so much to see that exhibitions blur

into one; where Lind queues and sweats, I squeeze (or am squeezed) through crowds and displays, eventually flag, and feel bleary.

If not now, then when? Because I am a viewer piecing together (in theory) fragments of intent or a theme, I never know or see the full idea that stretches over and across shows. I get confused in the gaps between one exhibition and the next, trying to mentally connect a narrative that I am never certain actually exists. At *GEO-DESIGN: Junk — All that is solid melts into trash* at the VanAbbemuseum, a show of work by DAE alumni about consumer culture and the remnants of design, I learn about global recycling chains and their failures, silicate waste, the refusal of nation states to take responsibility for space debris... I am not asked to 'solve' any issue — these are things much bigger than me, as a person, as a designer — but to question my own behaviours in relation to these things. In *The Isolated System of Junk in Gaza,* Ines Glowania documents the routes that are taken to dispose of household rubbish under Israel's blockade, through interviews and maps drawn by Gaza's residents. While goods can still be imported in, refuse systems have collapsed. Rubbish can't get — or isn't allowed — out. Convenience becomes a luxury as existing landfills reach capacity. Junk isn't only presented as something that is designed — it is something that also has embedded geographies and social, political, and economic ideologies and relations. (Back at home, I think about these pen-drawn diagrams often, remembering the journeys and politics they refer to nearly every time I take my own bin out.)

Seeing this exhibition first left me with expectations for what would follow, and vulnerable to the kind of disappointment that Lind describes. I had hoped for interrogation like the identity suggested. Also at Dutch Design Week: designer-makers create and show off things made out of bioplastics, which make new problems while claiming to solve old ones; trade show-type displays touch lightly on economic sustainability; Dutch Invertuals round up a decade with an exhibition that is exquisitely made but seems totally unrelated and exclusively celebratory; there are several shows of student work — work that is beautiful, but generally challenges politely, or is given a pass to sit outside of meaningful critical examination because youth is so often considered an exemption like that. (Exceptions include Mona Alcudia's *Peacock Chair* at the DAE show, which uses the 1970s icon to investigate the economy and labour around design, the chair's origins woven through with Filipino prison labour, and the work of students at the Vlisco®Co stand at Veem.) *If not now, then when?* wobbles and dislocates between one show and the next. Strategic and funding partners change between shows, swayed by the agendas of stimulus funding and 'talent development.' At *The Object is Absent,* a performative exhibition, designers and audiences try to negotiate the intentions of design that are left in the spaces once the object is taken away. It seems like a riddle. Designers look to the world that design has designed, and hope to find inspiration or something new. 'Can we find fresh perspectives on the relations between objects and us?' asks the introduction. 'Zero waste, no inequality!' Pep and exclamations fill in and make smooth the craters left by GEO-DESIGN's excavation of urgent complexity.

In fact, so little of Dutch Design Week worries about design as a direct contradiction to questions of change or sustainability that I start to wonder whether it is me (not design) who has missed the point, or if I am thinking too parochially. After three days, I am worn out from walking, and seeing, from being asked incessantly about the future, not knowing the answer, and not finding it anywhere in the things that are on display.[7] I give up, and reason to myself that somebody else — somebody much cleverer than I am — will figure it out. I leave feeling hopeless. Having imagined radicality or visions of complex and collaborative long term-ism, maybe pilots that I could engage with, I really don't know what to do with the Design, the capital-D kind on show, that neatly ties itself up in captions, or entertains, or performs until closing time.

Maybe submission in the face of overwhelm is the point. In a 2013 essay, writing about the Sharjah Biennial and the broader refusal of Middle Eastern biennials to adopt the 'fair-haired' style of thinking that had appeared and remained in Europe, semiotician Walter Mignolo is critical of the way that Western events worry themselves over status. Instead of thinking about what events at scale do, or could do, there is just 'an anxiety to be the 'newest' and a fear of being 'behind." (Mignolo, 2013) What is important isn't progress or empowerment that comes through and beyond the event, but for events — and cities — to be associated, however minimally, with wa checklist of 'right' subjects. The environment is one such 'right' subject, and having a cultural moment in and around design. Similar positions or questions repeat through recent events: *Design in Alert,* the 2017 Santiago Design Biennial; *Everything Was Forever, Until It Was No More,* the first Riga Biennial, and *Contour 9: Coltan as Cotton,* in Mechelen, Belgium, in 2018; *Design For Sustainability* at Shenzen Design Week in 2019; Bio-26, the 26th Biennial of Design held in Ljubljana, Slovenia, in 2020... But the concerns themselves aren't new. At the very least, these questions have repeated in parallel alongside the development of modernism since the mid-century. Each time, old questions are refreshed by new aesthetics. This time, shaped by millennial tastes, they are asked with leafy minimalism, neon green branding, and constructed in particle board and laminated ply.

By the time I leave Eindhoven, I'm no closer to an answer. I am also no clearer, really, on what I was being asked to begin with. Repetition and overwhelm are in fact key aspects of keeping things as they are, Mignolo writes, so that a hierarchy is perpetuated through the act of exhibiting. Like the gold-edged volumes of 1851, there are 'experts' who produce Design: the curators; the designers whose work is included; the judges who give out awards and medals. And then there are 'non-experts': the designers with less distinction or whose work doesn't behave nicely in a gallery; the non-designers; the people, like me, who get stuck in the gaps and inconsistencies between one exhibition and the next; the chronically overwhelmed. 'Experts' know what they are talking about. They define not only the content but the *terms* of the conversation: what is 'knowledge'? What can it be? What about design, and how is it linked to today's particular theme?

'Non-experts' — not so much.

But 'experts', focussing in on the details, tend not to ask the bigger questions about what their work actually supports: the environmental impact of exhibitions that appear for a week, or two, then disappear; the people who fly in and out; the financial sustainability, not viable by themselves and so propped up by commercial sponsors who stamp their logos across websites and guides as a show of corporate responsibility... Dutch Design Week, and others like it, are easily unravelled — by an uncritical commitment to form and tradition, again by ever expanding scales that work against discourse, and finally by novel and ever-changing subject matter. Discussions that are had so that they can be seen to have happened, move on to the next topic before finding depth, substantial progression, or a measurable point of conclusion. *If not us then who? If not now, then when?* Unanswerable and vague, the questions are as Teflon as the events themselves, protecting design from a kind of existential collapse. The 'problem' is elsewhere, outside, with someone else. Not with design itself. Or design events themselves. Not with their way of being, or 'knowing', with what they value or sustain and what they don't, or the way that complex issues are oversimplified and reduced to passing interests, momentarily urgent questions that are packed away during closing week. Glossy press shots and catalogue descriptions and digital remnants are all that is left over — nothing of the 'discourse' that did or did not happen. (Not existing is convenient like that. It is impossible to question the value of something that was never recorded.) The conversations that are had once and in fragments then disappear forever.

To be clear: *Dutch Design Week* is not, in any way, alone. It is one of many design events that repeat across Western Europe, unknowingly manifested out of centuries of history. It is not an easy timeline to span, though, connecting between two worlds that, for the most part, are unrecognisable from one another.

Local contexts and histories feel more tangible, and easier to track backwards. Eindhoven's history, for many, is tied up with the invention and design of carbon filaments and radio tubes and, from the late nineteenth century on, Philips — of incandescent lightbulbs, later extending out into x-rays, radio, and television — had been based in the city.[8] After playing a major role in the region's industrial history, Philips moved production to China in the 1970s and 80s, as manufacture followed lower financial remuneration of labour. The operational headquarters moved shortly afterwards, in 1997, to Amsterdam, leaving Eindhoven to become 'a ghost town' (Martin, 2018) haunted by capitalism.

Faced with the tail-end of free-market policies, the city stepped in. The first 'Day of Design' took place in 1998 as an opportunity for designers and entrepreneurs to network, hoping to massage both industry and the economy back to life. Over time, the event increased in size and length to the 'Week of Design' in 2002, before being renamed again in 2005 to include the whole of the Netherlands. Alongside this, strategic long-term moves were made to position Eindhoven as 'one of the world's top creative innovation regions.' In 2012, these buzzwords were formalised into a marketing organisation — Eindhoven 365 — and, the following year, the electric stripes of a logo appeared. The city, like others in Europe around the same time, had transformed. Three jagged stripes had created what designer and critic Ruben Pater calls 'a three-day destination'. (Pater, 2018) Eindhoven now had a new identity, and was marked by this logo as a location worth visiting. Eindhoven (the brand) and Eindhoven 365 are now the primary Strategic Partners of Dutch Design Week; the event effectively becoming marketing collateral, more one part of a set of branded assets that activate and smooth out a civic identity, than anything about design.

'At minimum,' says a friend, who is also a designer, as we talk about these events, 'it's a nice opportunity to go away.' He visits Venice most years. Between us, we forget that travel is a luxury, and that time left over is a luxury, too. It is not uncommon to compact a holiday and work-ish things together; as I research, more than one person asks me if I am going to become 'one of those people who jets off all over the world, visiting all of the design places.' From what I can gather, 'world' really means the cities, two hours or so from London, that compete for the attention and remaining holiday days of short haul audiences. Budget airlines redraw cartographies, once formed around railways as profitable arcs through the air, recentring Europe in the process.

As cities try to differentiate themselves from one another, visualising their local contexts into outward identities, they are not (it turns out) too dissimilar from place to place. In late-November 2019, about a month after I visit Eindhoven, I fly to Portugal to catch the end of Porto Design Biennale: *Post Millennium Tension*. The triangle that I trace between three imperial histories is accidental but not, from my London centre, entirely unpredictable. Now that empires have largely collapsed, Western Europe competes with itself for the recognition of 'culture' seekers and the capital they bring with them. From September until December, Porto Design Biennale takes over historic and repurposed sites across the city and nearby port-town, Matosinhos. The biennial, which is publicly funded by the councils of both municipalities, has a huge overall budget — €1.6million — and is expected to attract 100,000 visitors. (Later numbers suggest that, in the three months of the biennial, about 50,000 extra international visitors came to the city.)

Like Eindhoven, Porto Design Biennale fits into an ongoing city-wide agenda. In 2014, a rebrand turned Porto from a city into: *Porto.* Porto — full stop. The logo is white and blue, like the azulejo tiles that cover the city and end up on Instagram, and has been turned into sculptures that tourists can have their photo taken next to, as proof that they have been. Porto Design Biennale takes over as Portugal's main design event following, without interruption, eighteen years of the EXD Biennale, established in Lisbon by experimentadesign, which collapsed in 2017. The wider civic strategy that the biennial fits within is not hidden from visitors — it's proudly announced. 'Design has emerged in recent years as a key discipline for thinking about the city and building its future,' writes Rui Moreira, who is both Chairman of the Board of Porto Design Biennale and Mayor of Porto, in the programme that accompanied the biennial's opening week. 'This international phenomenon is particularly important in Matosinhos and Porto, two cities that have brought design practice into the centre of their cultural strategy, not limiting its potential to the artistic field, but using it continuously as a catalyst for social, economic, technological and environmental change.'

Rather than posing a question, *Post Millennium Tension* is divided into three lines of enquiry: 'Present Tense', a survey of the last fifteen years of design; 'Design and Democracy', exploring the 'deliberate creation of relationship modes between ourselves and others' through design; and 'Design Forum', a series of events questioning and reflecting on design. Each strand of exploration seems too big to cover fully. But by the time I arrive, although the cities are still highlighted by the yellow identity, still bright as autumn and the weather begin to turn, the biennial has already begun to wind down. Most of what is left are the Satellite events that exist outside of the main theme, so I never really feel as though I know what the biennial reveals. *Millennials: New Millennium Design*, the main exhibition seen by approximately 20,000 visitors, has shut. *Design Systems* and *Portugal Industrial: Links Between Design and Industry* both closed weeks before I arrived. I look through the window of MMIPO as the Riccardo Dalisi show is packed away. Some of guest country Italy's events are still open, although what Italy actually offers as a guest country never feels completely articulated. I visit *Frontiere -- Expressions of Contemporary Design* at Casa do Design, an exhibition described as a display of how Italian designers, 'reacting to the stimuli of the post-millennium reality, are discovering new dimensions in approaching design', and find myself disappointed in the same way as I was in Eindhoven by a surface level of interrogation. Later on, I go to *Abitare Italia: Icons of Italian Design* at the Palácio das Artes and come out less jostled and bruised than I did Dutch Design Week. Unlike Eindhoven, my version of Porto Design Biennale is much quieter and less crowded than the press shots. The invigilator and I are the only people there, and our shoes squeak after one another on the polished floors. Design is presented as silent objects on plinths, their histories as uncomplicated, and summed neatly up into captions. I take a selfie in an Ettore Sottsass *Ultrafragola* mirror that is on display (the most millennial thing I could do, it seems appropriate?), and wonder about the tension between an architect-designed mirror described as 'ridiculous' by its creator, and a renaissance caused by social media fifty years later.

Of the other exhibitions that are open, *Que Força É Essa — Protest and Democratic engagement in Portugal: Handmade Posters from the Ephemera Archive* brings together signs of protest around precarious work. The signs read in Portuguese, but the visual languages of companies that tangle themselves up with zero-hours contracts and gentrification are familiar: Uber, Facebook, Deliveroo... It documents a widespread moment of gig-economy frustration, captured through hand-drawn signs that were marched through streets. Later, after seeing Mário Moura's small and very good *A Força da Forma* at the municipal library — an experiment in juxtapositions, hoping to reveal something about the country's history and politics through graphic parallels in popular Portuguese books — I sit for a while in the open corridors and listen to the silence. Small and precise, it is the first time that I feel as though something specific to Portugal is explicitly revealed to me as a visitor, as well as to residents. I have been allowed into a private query between design and the context that surrounds it, a discussion I would never have been let in on, or known about, otherwise.

Over dinner, a friend tells me more about Moura's exhibit. 'These are books almost everyone has in their homes,' she tells me, 'so as a design exhibition, it's actually really accessible to anyone.' We talk about the shows and talks that she visited, which ones she thought were good. Also: about how much of our lives revolve around trying to be in a certain place at a certain time to catch events or — more often — managing to miss everything completely.[9] I think back to this conversation later, whilst reading Lind's critique of Venice. I enjoy Lind for how she takes in events at eye-level, a spectator herself. Critical concerns about content, or 'festivalisation', or tourism are raised through tangible experiences. When I try to piece together a judgment of Porto Design Biennale, my opinion slips through holes made by exhibitions I didn't, couldn't, see. What I visit is excited and proud, not often critical — of the discipline, of the format itself — but I doubt myself over the things that might have been a week or two ago. I wonder how many designers saw everything at the Biennale, then about how many non-designer residents did the same, then if that was the point at all. Somehow, missing out feels as overwhelming as seeing everything. As I research, I realise how much of these events depends on 'being there' — being physically present, but also having a body and mind that cooperate. There are dark spots on my memories of Porto, the things I didn't witness, and Eindhoven, the things I did, but were obscured by crowds of others, or lost in fatigue. I try the design press for reviews or documentation of other events, and come across interviews that take place prior to opening week, where curators and organisers talk about the aims and ambitions for their events. I search, but never

manage to find any follow ups, the same people publicly evaluating the event or its impact.[10] Everything I read is hyped up, fantastic. A kind of mysticism forms through word of mouth reviews from trusted colleagues: the shows that were good, the cities that can be relied upon in one way or another, the events that inherit ideas of criticality or pedagogy as they pass from the hands of one curator to another. Missing things makes it impossible to make an assessment with any confidence.

In the free-time that expands between closed shows, I do tourist things. I visit the São Bento railway station and read Portugal's history laid out in the tiled walls of the foyer; see the peacocks at the Jardins do Palácio de Cristal; walk from one side of the Luis I bridge to the other and back again. I visit the Monument Church of St Francis and the catacombs. When I buy too many pastéis de nata, I say 'obrigada' very shyly and quietly, with an awkward Midlands slant.

These are the details I like to hold onto best. Reading about cultural tourism, I find it easy to slip into political abstracts. Design events, the branded weeks and months that are stuck on top of a city, seem conceptually far away and abstracted by the literature. In these small moments, though, they become tangible; people show up on the other side. I remember that 'cultural tourist' means me. Also: the 2,000 Wolverhampton fans, some of whom are on the same flight as me from London Stansted, travelling through Porto to an away-game against Braga. What really is the difference? I recognise many of the same faces around the city, and again on the return journey. On their way through Porto, some of the fans cross paths with Belgian Standard Liege supporters — I see them in their jeans and black jackets, too — who are travelling to nearby Guimarães. The fights that break out make the news.

Cultural tourism assigns value to certain things. High-culture, which is classically White and middle-class, and definitely does not include football,[11] leads to the 'good' tourism that cities vie for through visual identities and public strategy.

It is quiet, and genteel, and has a certain set of behaviours attached to it. Fighting in the streets is not one of those. (Try to imagine a hundred artists or designers in a fist-fight, you'll see what I mean.) 'Good' tourism is the kind that is self-funded and conserves itself through the income injected into the economy; 'good' tourists are, by extension of implied morals, 'good' people.

This 'good' cultural tourism is pleasant at the time and smiles politely, learns enough of the language to say 'please' and 'thank you.' It happens without the immediate violence of broken glass and noses and blood-stained pavements. But it isn't violence-free; there is a creeping morbidity of enjoying a place whilst using it up. It is difficult to understand these kinds of politics as you enact them, though. Capital siphons almost directly from one metropolis to another, bypassing the provinces entirely. It pools in the 4+ star impressions made by Google or Trip Advisor reviews that recommend this restaurant over another, that bar above the rest. Spare rooms are advertised on Airbnb. Housing is bought up as second homes or holiday lets that stay empty in the off-season, hollowing the city out. Rent goes up. House prices go up. Gentrification is one sided like that, and one person's investment, in turn, prices another out of their basic need for shelter. Coffee shops and chains that force out small businesses and their owners are quick to follow. A visual identity that links last year's design event, with this year's, with next, hides the changes to the city that happen in between.

While I research these things, people tell me (mostly without me having to ask) about the events they love, the cities they love. For the same reasons that I get stuck on football fans and cultural tourism, I get stuck on trying to work out the difference between 'loving' a place and caring for it, and whether the former can happen without the latter. Writing in *Biennials/Triennials: Conversations on the*

Geography of Itinerant Display, an overview of architecture events, Léa-Catherine Szacka asks almost as an aside: 'Do people really care about the city when organising or visiting a biennial or triennial?' (Szacka, 2019, p. 30) The distinction is not a straightforward one, and one that I can't quite unpick until later. Love for a city turns out to be more of an abstract affection, an easy sentiment as a visitor passing through. Care, though, is where other people show up again. It is about avoiding harm. The issues that show up in Porto and Matosinhos are different, but not so much, from the ones that manifest in and around Shoreditch, around *Forests,* around London Design Festival. In his research into the emergence of design districts, the territories that form around design events, sociologist Ilpo Koskinen describes these places as 'semiotic neighbourhoods'. These places, Koskinen writes, symbolise design and an imagined lifestyle that design implies — linking right back around to high culture, tradition, and White middle-class-ness. 'When people and the media begin to recognise an area as a semiotic neighbourhood,' he writes, 'the area gains an enviable reputation.' (Koskinen, 2009, p. 3)

Semiotic neighbourhoods cut straight through 'care': idealising a place whilst ignoring the mundane realities and minutia of day-to-day local politics. Change isn't experienced abstractly by 'the city' — it's experienced by people. (The handmade signs of *Que Força É Essa* point to exactly that.) It is the aspirational symbolism of the Great Exhibition, only this time at street-level, on your doorstep. On *someone's* doorstep. The power shifts from countries, economies, and imports, to disposable income and which individuals benefit from, or are agents of, gentrification.

The question of care really becomes a question of whether it is possible to think about other people and their lives as you bisect them with your own — whether it is humanly possible to do this at the scale, in passing, but still with the inhabitant knowledge of a local.[12] More than once, I wonder about the people of Porto and Matosinhos, of Eindhoven, of Shoreditch, too: how residents feel about their home's 'enviable reputation', about D/design, the events that celebrate it, the changes and things that continue to impact daily life once the festival or biennial has been dismantled and taken away. Are the economic benefits that are used as justifications felt in significant or worthwhile ways? I find myself more interested in the qualitative evaluations of home owners and renters than the quantitative concerns of organisers and curators, but the problem, I realise, is that these things are difficult to capture without influence. Asking 'what do design events do for you?' positions everyone involved as either inside or outside of the churning cycle of design. An 'expert' or not. As a part of, or against, the progress these events infer. The civic argument of statistics has already been stacked in design events', and repetitions', favour. Not many people care about their city and would admit — by implication — to wanting it to be worse.

Fifteen months later, the complete rupturing of 'Real' and 'World' throws a breaker into this circuit. Hastily put together panel discussions fill the gap left by events that don't happen. Time opens up and, in this interruption, space is created to consider what these events do or don't do, whether they fulfil their claims and expectations, if there are alternatives. What these alternatives might be, exactly — organisers and curators aren't quite sure. Instead they speak about the new challenges of organising biennials and festivals that are 'blended', simultaneously online and offline, as though we hadn't been living across these spaces for a decade or more.

Watching these conversations, I wonder whether another option had, perhaps, already been presented, hidden within a biennial itself. In *Pessimism of the Intellect, Optimism of the Will: Optimism & Foresight* (2019), the first edition of the journal that goes with, and is planned to continue after Porto Design Biennale, curator José Bártolo describes the quality he sees in millennial design(ers) that he considers to be event-worthy as a topic. Resistance and protest are key, he writes, sitting somewhere between direct action and artistic creation. Bártolo calls this 'optimism as a political category.' He writes:

> '...resilient optimism tends to be a trait associated with the Millennial generation, as if they were the best generation prepared to "stop surviving", using the words of André Barata: "When I say that the most revolutionary thing we can do is stopping, what I'm saying is that stopping is the most effective way to question a system of social domination that relies on acceleration. And, for that reason, it's also probably the hardest thing to achieve."' (Bártolo, 2019, pp. 11-12)

'Stopping entirely' was the kind of design thought-experiment I had expected to be presented with at Dutch Design Week. Like the recycled *If not now then when?*, the sentiment isn't new, paraphrasing poet and writer Gary Snyder's 1970 assertion 'the most radical thing you can do is stay at home.' And I assumed (wrongly) midway through 2020, that design events might trial stopping when Snyder's provocation became reality. What I hadn't anticipated was that designers might soothe themselves in trying to carry on. Divorced reluctantly from their cities, the events that remained were stripped of extravagance, confined to a browser window that made content and relationships clearer. The first of these came early on, in April, in a video uploaded to YouTube: filming in the dark, a man puts a key into the lock of a door, turns it four times clockwise — *ker-chunk, ker-chunk, ker-chunk, ker-chunk* — and pushes open the door. The video cuts to a fusebox. The trip switches are flipped back on; the interior of a bar lights up. It is empty, except for the man and the chairs that sit patiently at tables. Turning the camera around and towards himself, the man smiles and says, 'Hello, my name is Maurizio Stocchetto, owner of Bar Basso.' The camera pans across the untended bar, up to a chandelier. 'With the *Dezeen Virtual Design Festival,* we still have a chance to stay together.' He signs his brief introduction off with a 'big hug', and the video cuts 600 miles north-west from Milan to London. At arm's length and waist height, looking down into the camera, Marcus Fairs, *Dezeen's* editor-in-chief, replies asynchronously. 'Thanks Maurizio. We're really going to miss you this year and we look forward to seeing you and all of our friends at Bar Basso again next year.'

Maurizio is swiftly followed by a roll-call of designers, who talk one by one about their hopes for the digital festival. I am not sure what to make of the video. I notice that I care less about the designers, but go between various feelings of concern for Stocchetto, his shuttered bar, and the impact that a missing summertime peak in design tourism will have, through tempered positivity about the benefits of being online that might make events just a little bit more accessible, then back to unease at the brutality of a cut screen that leaves Stochetto and Bar Basso behind. *Virtual Design Festival,* briefly named Virtual Milan, fills a hole in *Dezeen's* annual reporting that usually revolves around Milan Design Week. It tries hard to mimic real life from the start, unimaginatively so, and falls into a predictable pattern of there being too much and trying to cater for too many. Amongst other things, the Festival includes: carouselling images of graduate projects, to fill in the gaps left by cancelled end of year shows; practitioner talks and portfolio shares; an awkward social space, as people try to navigate non-verbal cues of tiled conversations had through a screen; studio profiles; collaborations with brands like Vitra and partnerships with other cancelled events, *What Design Can Do* for one, all filed together in the same space; an attempt to react quickly to the Black Lives Matter movement with critical discussions about decolonising design; tentative moves towards platforming ideas and practitioners across timezones and continents with the help of fibre-optics... And, like real life events, some content is fascinating — a couple of talks, introductions to research projects (that, in their reporting, don't feel as though they've been done justice), manifesto videos recorded by collectives that pull apart current practice easily, and visibly delight in doing so. What is good provides enough cover for the advertising, so for a moment I forget that my attention is being bought and sold to the sponsors and partners whose names hyperlink out. When it wanders, I can leave and come back. A mandated move online means that everything can be asynchronous, including the live talks that are recorded and made available on demand, easily paused for a moment or subtitled. There are parts I go back to months later, filling in the dark spots of things I forgot or didn't catch at the time. As *Virtual Design Festival* archives itself for a later date, access requirements are considered by accident and in the smallest of ways, designers thinking about ways to connect as their own movements are restricted, rather than out of any real desire to be inclusive.

Ultimately, I find myself feeling overwhelmed by volume, again, and disappointed overall. The content is mainly architecture- and product-driven, and light on context. (I wonder privately what else I expected.) This time around, disappointment feels sharper. Time has a renewed sense of preciousness; it is no longer a concept that stretches out, apparently forever. I am reminded of life's fragilities daily by the same news reports that tether me back to London. My time has currency and needs budgeting so as not to waste it — which turns out not to be as easy as it sounds as more and more events happen online and missing things becomes easier than ever. Perhaps the thing we will remember about this period is not the quality of the things that happened and were consumed, but the quantity, as people distracted themselves away from contemplating their own mortality. Some weeks later, when I talk to Salem Al-Qassimi, founder of the Fikra Graphic Design Biennial, we catch on this point and how quickly interest in online content subsequently waned. A year prior to the pandemic, thinking about the shape of the 2020 event, Al-Qassimi had wondered whether the event needed to happen in real life. 'As we were putting together the second biennial, we had to think about the first — what worked what didn't work, what was missing... There was this notion of just thinking about the way the world works today, and that maybe a physical location is not necessarily something that we need to prioritise. Maybe it's digital. Maybe it could be a little bit more global via the internet,' he tells me. 'When the pandemic happened, it felt like it was very relevant, although now I think there are just so many online things that it feels a bit...' He trails off. There is a difference between wanting to be online and having to be.

Held in 2018 in Sharjah, the third-most populous city in the United Arab Emirates, the inaugural Fikra Graphic Design Biennial began with three aims: to provide a platform for designers within the UAE to participate in global discourse on graphic design; to conduct research related to graphic design; and, to question the role of the graphic designer today. Called *The Ministry of Graphic Design*, the biennial was produced under the artistic direction of Prem

Krishnamurthy, Emily Smith, and Na Kim, and organised into a structure that described the UAE's administration. 'The government in the UAE is extremely forward thinking in terms of Ministerial structures,' says Al-Qassimi. 'So we have the Ministry of Artificial Intelligence, the Ministry of Climate Change, a Minister of Tolerance, a Minister of Happiness.' A Ministry of Graphic Design that researched the potential in and of the discipline was not at all unbelievable.[13] (Al-Qassimi tells me that the blue and white signage that fronted the former Bank of Sharjah, the building borrowed for the event that had been due to be demolished, convinced a number of passers-by so much that they came in to see what was going on.) Each of the six 'Departments' cracked open the subject in different ways. The *Dept. of Graphic Optimism,* curated by Alia Al-Sabi, told a visual history of the UAE through printed ephemera produced and distributed during the 1970s and 80s, as well as showcasing the work of the prolific Hisham Al Madhloum; common-interest's *Dept. of Non-Binaries* expanded 'design' into 'designerly', collecting together a range of practices that shared a way of thinking, broadening the subject and its outputs; the *Dept. of Mapping Margins,* led by Uzma Z Rizvi, explored a critical future for graphic design through the lens of anthropology, considering the subject alongside strategies of commensality, decolonising and decentring. The *Office of the Archive,* produced by Tetsuya Goto and Saki Ho, kept record. While publications that are released after an event tend to keep track of a biennial line of thought (see, for example, *Are We Human?* by Beatriz Colomina and Mark Wigley, continuing the questions asked during the 3rd Istanbul Design Biennial, or *Crack Up, Crack Down,* an examination of satire in Slovenia, following the 33rd Ljubljana Biennial of Graphic Arts in 2019, curated by Slavs and Tartars), the *Office of the Archive* approached documenting the first Fikra

Graphic Design Biennial differently, asking questions about what these kinds of events have to offer.[14] The biennial is reimagined in fragments and from multiple perspectives; embracing the one-to-one scale of viewership, it avoids retelling, and captures the thoughts of visitors but also participants, curators, and organisers, through staged press shots and candid Instagrams. Instead of a linear commentary, Goto and Ho use the issue to continue to research into '"impressions" and "perceptions" of graphic design', embedding their archive with multiple histories in the process.

Photos of the building capture beautiful, layering metaphors. Originally built in the 1970s by Spanish architects Tecnica y Proyectos, the modernist bank is one of 17 almost identical blocks and stood derelict, a form without function, swirling with calligraphic graffiti by French-Tunisian street artist eL seed. Ultimately, it would be rejuvenated by the biennial, and become full with graphic design that challenged the potency and relevance of Western practices, movements, and ideologies. Held in November, in between other design events happening in the city, the Fikra Graphic Design Biennial was deliberately educational, a non-commercial counterpoint. It wasn't a poster show, or a competition, or a display of Photoshopped outcomes, nor was the ambition to increase footfall or promote the host city. It is a longer term strategy that focusses on the discipline and the people of the region — not economy. 'I think there needs to be a commercial event, but I think it's healthy to have these alternatives as well. If there are only commercial events, then what's the point? It's healthy to have these alternatives so that you can start to critique. You're able to see what's working, what's not working.' Privately-funded and financed by Fikra (Al-Qassimi's studio), the Ministry of Graphic Design had the kind of freedom and autonomy necessary to make that decision. (Beyond support in terms of logistics, he tells me that there was relatively little intervention from the local government.) It is also why, at time of writing, a second event hasn't yet happened. Financial autonomy is not easy, and is made more difficult as potential backers worry about their own short- and long-term financial futures. But there is also no rush or civic rhythm to keep pace with, no year on year contracts and commitments to uphold, regardless of whether it is safe to do so or not.

When I ask him about success, it's the three original aims Al-Qassimi refers back to, how much of each was achieved — not numbers or statistics. 'The metrics are sometimes important for sponsorship, but for me that's not success.' He tells me that, since the event, opportunities opened up for designers in the region to collaborate and work globally. It's a difficult thing to calculate, a slow-burning change, and arguably not too far removed from the 'networking' essence of Dutch Design Week, or the regional and national focus of Porto Design Biennale. What is different is that, in rejecting Western ways of doing and thinking and being, the Fikra Biennial deliberately pulls the industry into wider, not tighter, circles. 'I hope it continues to connect people from different places,' he says, 'and that the designers from this part of the world aren't considered "outsiders" in terms of graphic design.'

Either side of our discussion of the biennial, we talk about relishing in enforced introversion, about our experiences of teaching, and about doubt, too. I mention that I increasingly wonder about being unsure as a necessary part of teaching, an uncertainty that grows in line with experience, never feeling entirely comfortable in presenting information without a caveat. In the UAE, Al-Qassimi says, graphic design doesn't have the same established career profile that might be present elsewhere. 'It's a very new and abstract discipline... it's also usually considered as a hobby, not a career path,' he says. The events that happen around Fikra present graphic design as unequivocally commercial as a way to claim value. So there is added pressure on the biennial to open the subject up — to designers and non-designers, but also to uncertainty and the possibility inherent within it. 'A platform that speaks on behalf of graphic design is a huge responsibility,' he says, 'because you're not just talking about the discipline, you're portraying what *you* think about it.'

As we talk about the Fikra Biennial, Al-Qassimi tells me more about what future events might cover. It is important, he says, that future biennials explore topics with particular relevance to the region, and are not conversations that could be placed anywhere. He and the board of directors would consult internally, then with other practitioners in the region, deciding on the things that needed to be or weren't being addressed. Accountability is communal. It is not — should not — be one persons' topic to decide. Only then would a curator be approached; they would be asked to respond to the given subject, rather than present their own interest as a theme. Because of this, he tells me, it's also important that this person is a practicing designer and educator, not just a curator. Pedagogy and praxis are fundamental parts of the event.

In the weeks that follow, I play over Al-Qassimi's comments on doubt and responsibility in my mind. Some of the hasty panel discussions mention the ethics of spending public money in times of crisis or impending recession, or the extent to which design events really matter to the fabric of society. No one mentions the hard-to-do 'stopping entirely.' Instead, contributors snag on (design) community, inspiration, and the social contact that comes through these bigger events, the intimacies lockdowns have wiped out. Empathy and close contact are major topics across disciplines in what is left of 2020's events: *Empathy Revisited* at Istanbul Design Biennial, Manifesta 13's *Traits D'Union.s* in Marseille, *Come Closer* at the Biennial Matter of Art, Prague... Having presumably solved (or gotten bored by) *If not us, then who? / If not now, then when?* type questions, Dutch Design Week moves on in 2020 to explore *The New Intimacy.* Everyone says that they are desperate to hug one another again. The parties and social spaces and travel opportunities that come wrapped up with design events take over conversations.

The closest I get to a clear distinction between events happens in June, when the rescheduled London Design Festival is announced. Unlike London Design Festival, the third London Design Biennial has been pushed back. Citing international travel restrictions, more damaging to the Biennial than the Festival in terms of spectators, but also bringing in exhibitors and works, it will now happen in 2021.[15] *Resonance,* curated by Es Devlin, is so broad that the thematic edges disintegrate to include everything and nothing, and leaves room for a last minute nod to the pandemic. Another recycled question is now an open call: *Design in an Age of Crisis* — 'How can we create healthier, greener, equal and prosperous societies?

I find myself questioning, though, whether design is really capable of finding these solutions, and if it is — why has it not already? What is not mentioned in the Biennial's call out is the ways in which design has not only passively contributed to, but has been an active driving force in, creating unhealthy, unsustainable, unequal, and impoverished societies. 'Crisis' is framed as a series of unfortunate coincidences, not a 'Real' that we have created for ourselves. There is no doubt, no uncertainty, only unwavering confidence in design's ability to 'fix'.

Any ontology of design is ignored. Escobar, though, is very clear about the cause and effect relationship of practice. '[D]esign has been inextricably tied to decisions about the lives we live and the worlds in which we live them, even if this awareness seldom accompanies "design as usual." (Escobar, 2018, p. 33) The 'Real' and 'World' we occupy now — the 'Crisis' — can be traced back, rewinding through Enlightenment thinking and the design that came with it, to the beginnings of 'the suppression, devaluing, subordination, or even destruction of forms of knowledge and being that do not conform to the dominant form of modernity.' (Escobar, 2018, p. 94) He warns that we have to be conscious of 'the effects of a "tradition" in orienting people (including designers') ways of thinking and being.' (Escobar, 2018, p. 80) What he is advocating for, I realise, is uncertainty in our ways of knowing. But also uncertainty in design, as far as it exists in Eurocentric retellings, and its resolute proclamations of 'progress.'

Looking back through the stories of historic design events, buried under accounts of spectacle, I come across an entirely different history of the Great Exhibition that is prompted by a single object and undermines any confidence in large-scale European events to think holistically. Having made her London debut a few years earlier, Hiram Powers' wildly popular *Greek Slave* stood in the East Nave, red velvet curtains separating her from the rest of the USA's display. Carved into Serravezza marble, she is shackled at the wrists, nude and self-consciously on display, trying to not catch the eye of those around her. The Greek War of Independence had ended twenty years earlier, and Powers had written his statue a backstory, a life of servitude to the Ottoman Empire, around that fact. It is important to note, though, that it is 1851. Romantic and, importantly, literally White, it was up to audiences, as to how they perceived this woman. Viewers could choose, art historian Charmaine Nelson writes, to make the not too dramatic mental leap and confront the ongoing relationship that the USA had with slavery. They could consider the proud displays of wealth and power around them, and wonder what Britain or the Industrial Revolution would have been were it not for labour by enslavement and the annexation of half the world. Or — defended from critical accountability by the colour of her material skin — they could deny this narrative entirely. (Nelson, 2007) The space to do this was left deliberately by the Exhibition. Early on in the organisation of the event, abolitionists called for an unflinching examination of the Exhibition's relationships with slavery to be an integral part of the show; it was crucial, they argued, to understanding the contexts that surrounded items on display. These calls were ignored, as organisers tried to deemphasise the very direct link between 'progress' and the horrors of slavery.

In spite of this, the sculpture still prompted widespread public critique, and visitors struggled with the gap between the celebration of manufacture and its social and political reality. Anti-slavery protests, already common, began to centre around the statue. First, a woodcut illustration by John Tenniel appeared in *Punch* magazine, titled *The Virginia Slave,* drawing a direct and critical comparison to the real and present politics of America. Then, Powers' *Greek Slave* became an unwitting participant in institutional critique. Having escaped from North American slavery themselves, William Wells Brown and William and Ellen Craft had been touring Britain, and become popular figures lecturing the case for abolition. After several visits to the Great Exhibition, the three planned an intervention around the USA's stand. On June 21, underneath the American flag, Wells Brown, the Crafts, and other abolitionists, performed a mock auction, demonstrating to the British public the precursor to the wealth on display. Overseen by the *Greek Slave,* the performance saw Ellen Craft 'sold' by Wells Brown, a living counterpoint to Powers' inanimate fantasy. Tenniel's condemnatory illustration was displayed, unofficially, next to the statue. 'I place this *Virginia Slave* by the side of the *Greek Slave,*' said Wells Brown at one point, holding Tenniel's illustration in his hand, 'as its most fitting companion.' (Merrill, 2015, p. 145)

'Once in the modern period,' Escobar writes, 'the world comes to be increasingly built without attachment to place, nature, landscape, space and time — in short, without reference to the here and now.' (Escobar, 2018, p. 12) In their critique of the new institution of exhibition at scale, Wells Brown and the Crafts' performance bought back the 'here and now'. They bought complexity to the objects that had been put on pedestals, their stories flattened by 900,000 square feet of glass panels that separated them from the world outside.

That this critique was flattened later by the same pageantry is maybe not a surprise. Celebratory histories are the ones we know best; the ones that are told loudest and most triumphantly are also told by a country that has never examined the ways in which it did and undid the world. And so I wonder what this means for an open call around 'Crisis.' What 'Real', what 'World', and what 'Design' is it looking for? Would the Biennial even be capable of celebrating work that threatened to undermine its own history entirely?

This alternative history presents a question that I keep finding myself stuck on: where might we be now had the Great Exhibition and its fraternal peers unpicked the 'Real' and the 'World' that existed around showcasing and the showcased? What if 'Design' had held on to multiple meanings, and rejected its use a symbol of 'progress'?

The Great Exhibition, but also its massive and spectacular history — the single story that silenced its critics — exemplify a condition that Tony Fry calls 'defuturing': the systematic 'negation of futures.' (Fry, 1999, p. 10) Defuturing is the type of decision making that sees short-term gains, in this case: defining 'progress', political flexing, and attention seeking at a large scale, prioritised over the mid- and long-term losses they foreshadow. Short-term thinking, Fry writes, goes directly against sustainability (environmentally, but also politically, socially, culturally, economically.) By choosing to protect and value certain things over others, alternative outcomes becomes increasingly less possible. Rigid definitions of uncritical 'progress' that repeated soon boxed thought in, making it difficult, then impossible, to bridge the dissonance between holistic and relational practices and the context-lite obsessions of Europe and the West.

Any broader responsibility or impact (or care, for that matter) associated with decision making is often avoided, he continues, by claiming that it is impossible to know the future. 'That the future is made by actions in the past and present, and is then destined to travels towards us, escapes consideration.' (Fry, 1999, p. 10) Defuturing, though, is a concept that threatens the world with epistemic collapse, because it starts off a chain of hypothetical of questions. Because: what if organisers had valued the views of abolitionists, and encouraged context and critique? What if — at any point — the wider public had challenged what was presented to them? Or demanded accountability? What if, instead of stocktaking, the Great Exhibition had looked at itself as a moment of collaboration, that held each knowledge system in the same regard? The trajectories of these questions are impossible to know. But as these speculations split off in multiple directions of possibility, they reveal the alternatives that could have been, were designed out, prevented in the future by decision making at the time.

Like Fry, Mignolo sees shrunken and confined imagination as a direct result of rational modernity. '[T]he reason for the prevailing chaos,' he writes, 'is the persistence of global coloniality and the global conditions created in the advancement of Westernization.' (Mignolo & Wannamaker, 2015, p. 15) For him, meditation on this point isn't something that can be expected of chaos' myopic and 'fair-haired' creators. 'In order to change the terms of the conversation,' he writes, 'we ("the people") must start from the assumption that the West (the US, former Western Europe and their allies) can no longer offer solutions to the problems they themselves have created.' (Mignolo & Wannamaker, 2015, p. 19)

In June 2020, London Design Festival co-founder Ben Evans proves Mignolo's point succinctly and unselfconsciously. Talking about the event and its successes, Evans describes the landscape around the Festival as though its contextual power is some sort of happy accident:

> London's had some structural advantages. For one, we speak English, which is the global language of creativity. Two, we've had a world-beating education system that has attracted many people who have gone on to be stars of our sector. But, three, I think what we've got is the breadth and depth in London, which is unusual for a lot of cities, we're good at lots and lots of things. [...] Only last week I was interviewed by a Milanese journalist who described London as 'the creative capital of the world.' I kind of chuckled to myself [...] I just thought 'Oh my God — yeah! The message has got home. (Exposure London, 2020)

In his inability or refusal to acknowledge the history leading up to this point, Evans illustrates a survival tactic of modernity that Mignolo calls 'rewesternisation.' Capitalism and Western modernity are reasserted as a universal 'best option' for the majority of people. There is no discussion of why, or how, or what exactly 'best' means. They are detached entirely from wider systems of power and consequence, protecting key players in the process. Sometimes this happens through 'triumphant histories', like Evans' storytelling, or the selective memory of the Great Exhibition. Thinking back to Porto, I find myself wondering about the decision-making process — and its opacity — that chose Italy as an inaugural guest country, followed by France in 2021. Are the differences between Portugal and these countries, their (design) histories, enough to open the discipline up? Or are they so small as to clamp it more tightly shut? In Eindhoven: did the work that claimed to be radical ever really escape the desire and excess of neoliberalism — or just deflect attention from it? Rewesternisation, Mignolo notes, is pervasive exactly because it happens on these different scales. Most obviously, it shows up in the way that European countries pursuit of economy-first politics, leaning further and further to the political right since the turn of the millennium, though conservatism and on to nationalism, fascism, xenophobia and racism. In the United Kingdom, the public's decision to withdraw from the European Union (Brexit is one of the few things that manages to interrupt wall-to-wall news coverage of the pandemic) aggressively reasserted beliefs about modernity and coloniality. For half the country, notional ideas of empire, of a 'Great' Britain were reactivated yet again. For the other: disillusion. Where post-World War II Britain wobbled with debt, it is now faced with collapsing economic, diplomatic, and social relations.

In the end, London in September 2020 is not quite as 'filled with design' as it had claimed it would be. The Festival, like many other events, overpromised, too hopeful that the pandemic would end as quickly as it had begun. In real life, only four Design Districts — King's Cross, Shoreditch, Mayfair, Brompton, areas of London bloated and maintained by old wealth or new money — materialise, down from eleven the previous year, as U-turning legislation makes exhibiting difficult. The rest is mediated by screens. A series of talks and elliptical debates around design's relationship with the Circular Economy happen online. Three White men and one White woman, including the Executive Chair of IDEO and Chief Sustainability Officer of IKEA, lead the introductory talk. Epistemic questions about whether these people want, or can imagine, or should be platformed in relation to radical change are never asked. A 'Virtual Design Destination' by Adorno, described as a 'digital-first online gallery' gives viewers the opportunity to 'travel' and view works rendered into fourteen European 'locations': resting on the seabed in Finland; floating on pedestals of Icelandic sea ice; Estonian design placed into sand dunes and buffeted by wind; Belgian work digitised into an imagined Magritte set... Each of the virtual exhibitions are sponsored by tourism boards, embassies, and Government established culture and creativity initiatives, who sticker logos on to work in anticipation of a future where much-needed cultural tourism can resume.

The mistake, I think, is to consider the compacted and mainly digital London Design Festival — or any design event, for that matter — as a one-off, or small enough not to worry about, or as something that just keeps bored designers occupied. None of these things happen in isolation. Decisions being made now reach beyond a cycle of events in 2021 or 2022; they either maintain or reject ambitions and philosophies that go forward. Over the course of the summer, I lose count of the times the 'New Normal' is mentioned, a quickly maligned phrase, as though a different version of the future will work itself out without much thought or discomfort. For design events, the reality is that more of the same is lined up. In 2018, the UK government announced plans for a 'Brexit Festival', extravagantly funded by £120million of public money. Running with the title Festival UK* 2022, the nationwide display of STEAM (Science, Technology, Engineering, Arts, Mathematics) outputs hopes to reconcile a United Kingdom that has been split, almost exactly, in half. (Youngs, 2020) On the website, flat-sided geometric type reads: *Open, Original, Optimistic.* 'Looking to a more hopeful and optimistic future through creativity. Confidence and positivity run through everything we do.' (Festival UK* 2022, n.d.) Having spent decades strategically stripping both the arts sector and education of funding, the government's Festival 2022 will develop and fund ten public commissions. Thirty 'creative teams' are currently involved. Obvious comparisons circle backwards through history: a governmental directive based in wishful-thinking; a country threatened by debt and economic collapse; design as a tool for promotion and investment; a desperate need to attempt to salvage some kind of political reputation at home and internationally...

   To ensure that the Festival succeeds — in diplomatic terms, as much as societal ones — at '[c]hampioning UK creativity,' (Festival UK* 2022, n.d.) it is being led by Chief Creative Officer Martin Green. Green comes with a proven track record and other business-loaded titles: Head of Ceremonies for the London 2012 Olympic and Paralympic Games, Director of Hull's year as the UK City of Culture in 2017. A near-copy of the EU-initiated Creative Europe scheme, the UK City of Culture comes off the back of Liverpool's success as European Capital of Culture in 2008, although 'success' I realise, sounds a lot again like gentrification. According to Creative Europe, becoming a Capital of Culture offers five 'value added' benefits:

'regenerating cities; raising the international profile of cities; enhancing the image of cities in the eyes of their own inhabitants; breathing new life into a city's culture; and, boosting tourism.' (European Commission, n.d.) Put another way: it is a contest for provincial cities and towns that have been systematically deprived to compete against one another on behalf of their residents. A winner is selected based on predetermined notions of culture. Merit follows merit, so this box ticking exercise helps secure further funding in the future. Really, very little is about 'culture' at all.

Festival UK* 2022 proposes the same value added, but on a national level. Some feel cautiously optimistic about the potential to do something positive and make change, particularly within the arts, but the overall commentary around the Festival shows the general lack of faith in these events to produce meaningful results. When art critics the White Pube, Zarina Muhammad and Gabrielle de la Puente, announce their role as advisors to the Festival's selection process on Twitter and Instagram, their followers are split — despite the pair's transparency over using this role to bring financial sustainability to their practice. It was 'hypocritical', some said. Others were supportive of their involvement and ambition to bring dynamic change from the inside out. At the same time, Migrants in Culture — a network organising for the safety of cultural workers working under and affected by the UK's Hostile Environment policies[16] — were working on an open letter rejecting the event. Addressed to Green, Neil Mendoza, the Commissioner for Cultural Recovery and Renewal, and Culture Secretary Oliver Dowden, Migrants in Culture described the Festival as a 'nationalistic project' (Migrants in Culture, n.d.) that used the devastation to the cultural sector, desperate for financial aid, as a vehicle to support xenophobic policy:

Festival UK* 2022 could have been an opportunity
for the UK's cultural sector to recognise the cognitive
dissonance that allows it to fabricate false-narratives
of 'openness' and 'optimism' while at the same time
mandating passport checks and making precarious
migrant workers redundant. We do not need a
festival claiming to 'bring people together' while
the government's Hostile Environment forces
people apart. We do not need a festival that seeks
to whitewash the UK's endemic racism using our
cultural capital. (Migrants in Culture, n.d.)

Migrants in Culture 'call for an immediate cancellation of
the festival and the reallocation of its £120 million budget
towards an equitable recovery for the arts and cultural
sector' (Migrants in Culture, n.d.) — a 'stopping entirely.'
Although the White Pube and Migrants in Culture occupy
slightly different positions, being inside and outside the
Festival,[17] what they both demand is an acknowledgement
of the defuturing that has taken place within the arts and
cultural sector, and the epistemic and real life violence that
this has resulted in.

What they are calling for is an interrogation of the
Festival's ontology. Because what if Festival UK* 2022 *was*
cancelled? What if we did stop, entirely, until these events
could be imagined in ways that valued culture — in all its
forms of knowing and being, its customs and practices, with
difference celebrated and integral — instead of using it as an
indication of 'power' and 'progress'? How might people and
values and, importantly, futures, plural, be designed in to
these events, instead of out?

'Imagine a culture sector coming together to support its most affected with a bold new approach to arts funding, employment, access and the running of the arts ecology,' the letter continues. 'A culture sector that champions diversity and brilliance, not only in branding statements but in concrete action and equitable distribution of funds and power across the country. Now that would be something to celebrate, don't you think?' (Migrants in Culture, n.d.)

As I read and reread the letter, I notice how changing the words 'arts' and 'culture' to 'design' reads similarly true. These are shared challenges, ones that reverberate through every aspect of life — beyond design, or arts, or STEAM subjects. Rethinking design and its events, comes with a particular sense urgency, though. It is not a question of importance, more one of ubiquity. '[D]esign is literally everywhere; from the largest structures to the humblest aspects of everyday life.' (Escobar, 2018, p. 2)

In a 2015 paper, Mignolo describes a process that he calls 'delinking': a disentanglement from ideologies and structures of power. It is an approach to reimagining the past-present-future that requires time, reflective action, and — more than anything else — commitment. 'It is a long process, at different levels and with different needs and preferences,' he writes. (Mignolo W. , 2017) Delinking, Mignolo writes, 'means that you become epistemically and politically disobedient, exposing the vulnerability and fictionality of what passes for "reality", and engaging, as many people on the planet already are, in rebuilding the communal.' (Mignolo & Wannamaker, 2015, p. 23) In Mignolo's delinked future, no place, or history, or knowledge system, is placed above another. A singular 'creative capital of the world' becomes more archaic the more I think about it. Likewise, a series of similar Capitals of Culture — or Design — that pass the title between themselves, trying the title on for a moment, before it is passed to the next. "The world today no longer needs one 'leader', and it is precisely this situation that is generating a domino effect in small states that still want to join the leader and in large states that do not want or need to be led any more." (Mignolo & Wannamaker, 2015, p. 19)

Mignolo does not see 'solutions' emerging from the West, where thought processes are too deeply entrenched. Change won't, for example, come about just by showcasing more of the work that unpacks the complexity of the world. Or siphoning off pocket-money amounts for the people whose city is performing, or for a cause that has caught attention.[18] It won't be bought about by well-intentioned White men and women organisers and curators platforming an increased number of practitioners who are also women of colour, or are non-binary, trans, disabled, or excluded in multiple ways, whilst still also controlling the terms of inclusion. Representation is, of course, undeniable in its value. But it can do very little on its own if the underlying structures of thought — what is valued, what is not — that run through these events aren't examined and dismantled. For Mignolo, the way that the West 'could and should play a crucial role' is by 'relinquishing the 'need' to lead the world.' (Mignolo & Wannamaker, 2015, p. 19) I think back to the conversations about inspiration, the panel discussions that tied themselves in knots trying to articulate the positives of events. Of course designers and design benefit from expanding notions of industry into wider, not tighter, circles. But there is a difference between an event filled with contextually embedded practice, that cherishes (a word that contains within it both love and care, but also protection) its relationships with the local, with the discipline, and one that competitively declares itself the world's best. These things are mutually exclusive. Getting from the one to the other requires a conceptual overhaul of the value system, starting from the basics: what 'Real', what 'World', what 'Design'?

Also, perhaps: Why 'Design' at all?

For Escobar and Fry, thinking about design (events) as a practice that rejects its embedded history of defuturing means 'destroying that which destroys': acknowledging — as delinking does — what design has prevented, and building the possibility of possibility into its future. Fry calls this far-sighted and holistic consideration *Sustainment* (as opposed to Enlightenment) thinking. Escobar, extending out this theory, calls for design to be *pluriversal* — to transition away from unsustainable neoliberal churning and towards degrowth, relational thinking, difference, mutual enhancement, autonomy... Both write that long-term thinking requires 'an explicit ethics of what to destroy and what to create, materially and symbolically'.

In other words: a framework of accountability. The very thing that 'design events', in their slipperiness, their cluttering together of biennials (examined in art and architecture) and festivals and weeks have never had. It comes with painful self-examination: What is it that these events *truly* sustain? What are their metrics of success, why do these things matter, and to whom? What might have value instead? And: what measurements might be taken to define 'success' as something that goes beyond dissolving curatorial statements of intent, and leaves behind bigness and footfall and economic wins? It is not the kind of inward and outward questioning that aligns with continuity or determination to 'lead.'

A framework that explores how an event acts on the people around it, the world, the understanding(s) of what design is and can be presents further questions: Who assumes accountability? Or regulates the events that don't, or chose not to, accommodate their wider publics? (I don't have answers to either of these.) Because what is difficult is that each of these theories require facing up to a hard truth: that Western design practices, as they refer back exclusively to their historic priorities are stagnating and getting smaller — despite and because of the events that get bigger and more expensive each year, desperately claiming otherwise. The kind of fundamental shift in thinking that might make them more meaningful is also the kind of fundamental shift that threatens to destabilise everything that has solidified around them. I return briefly to Bártolo's point: 'stopping is the most effective way to question a system of social domination.'

Would we lose much by stopping — or anything at all?

It strikes me that this is exactly the kind of existential discomfort these events have been trying hard to avoid. Escobar wonders if it is 'possible to reorient such a tradition and to redirect the journey into an altogether different direction? [...] Can design play a role in such a reorientation of both the cultural background and the journey itself?' (2018, p. 104) Transformative space has been created in the potential of the 'New Normal', and the gains could be huge: What if design events were reimagined with and for the people they have, up until now, excluded? What if 'a focus on the local' meant being reciprocal and communal, instead of a parachuted-in authority; could design be used as a way to excavate deeply and broadly, and make visible the complexity of that local? What if a design festival featured none of the things we have currently termed as 'design'? But these questions also require a huge amount of responsibility from the people who currently hold power; the kind of responsibility that Western Europe has not, traditionally, been able to evidence.

Are the organisers we have able to do this? As some kind of way out of the pandemic starts to feel close, tentative plans are made for 2021. Design events are very much back on the agenda from the start. Events are advertised to me on Instagram, the calendar is starting to block out once again: March has at least nineteen overlapping events, twelve of them design festivals, which emphasise much of what they did before.

'Travel from Sydney to Munich to Copenhagen with a minimal carbon footprint.' (Neon Moire, 2021) Either because, in the course of researching I have read them somewhere, or because over the course of the pandemic and lockdowns they feel achingly pertinent, I find myself turning over the final words of Samuel Beckett's *The Unnamable. I can't go on, I'll go on.* The third and most difficult book in a not-quite-trilogy, Beckett breaks narrative down almost to the point of unreadability. More poem than prose, the text barely resembles a novel. There is no clear sense of time, no plot or characters. What is left is a monologuing unnamed (unnamable) narrator, who windingly, maddeningly, questions his own existence. It is difficult to read, harder still to make any real sense of. Philosophers of various schools of thought attempted to claim *The Unnamable* for their own, each applying their own theories to make it more palatable, or seemingly about something — *anything* — despite the book's determination otherwise.

As I reread it, I draw a kind of parallel between *The Unnamable* and design events. With this third instalment, Beckett writes himself into a kind of creative and conceptual cul-de-sac. It is 'the ultimate point of paradoxical intensification,' writes Steven Connor in the preface, 'where narrative means have shrunk to nothing, but narration must go on, where there is nothing left to write with or about, and yet somehow the writing manages to continue, consumed by and subsisting only on itself.' (Connor, 2010, p. xviii)

There is something useful, I think, in this metaphor of *subsistence:* an idea that gone so far in on itself that it is fatigued and used up. A creative dead end. I think about the European design events that go round and around, repeating back on themselves, that feel like they are subsisting, too. Subsistence, I think to myself, seems like the most joyless future imaginable. It is not an outcome I associate with creativity. As I continue reading, the questions that repeated over and again at me lace their way in between the monologuing self-references, geeing up an exhausted conversation:

I can't go on.
    If not us, then who?
    If not now, then when?
        I'll go on.

and I'm struck by how easily I believe it.

[1] The pair were awarded CBEs for 'services to the creative industries' in 2008.

[2] When this news gets posted to Instagram, people are excited by the idea and write things in the comments like 'Great news!' and '▓ ▓ ▓' in spite of any specifics about how this will work. Later, it turns out that the Freelancer Portal is really a portfolio share, and less imaginative in its production than most of the graduate showcases that were hurriedly taken online.

[3] 'Fair' is also derived from the Latin *feriae* — holy days on which fairs were held — neatly tying commodities and production right back up with worship.

[4] *Ibid.* p. 53. Greenhalgh notes the extremity of domination at the time: 'The produce of every possession that could be economically transported was to be there... the East Indies, Indian Archipelago, Jersey, Guernsey, Ceylon [now Sri Lanka], Ionian Islands, Malta, Cape of Good Hope, Natal, West Coast of Africa, Canada, Nova Scotia, Newfoundland, New Brunswick, St. Helena, Mauritius, the Seychelles, St. Domingo, Grenada, Montserrat, St. Kitt's, Barbados, Antigua, British Guiana [now Guyana], the Bahamas, Trinidad, the Bermudas, South Australia, Western Australia, New Zealand, New South Wales, Van Diemen's Land [now Tasmania], Labuan and Borneo.'

[5] Escobar favours the term 'historicity' (historical authenticity) over 'history'.

[6] At points, I think I have found a distinction. While 'festivals' seem accepted as uncritical and celebratory, biennials are spoken about as sites or research, or criticality, or pedagogy, but when I look for evidence of this, I find inconsistency, as many exceptions to the rule as those that prove it.

[7] This makes more sense to me much later, when I see Dutch Design Foundation director, Martijn Paulen, talk about the DDW 2020 Open Call, in a discussion as part of Virtual Design Festival: 'As always with our theme, what we're trying to do is kind of catch the urgency of what's going on... But it's not a top-down theme. Designers don't have to relate to it. [...] You can just enter with good design, anyway.'

[8] Perhaps as a move to cement Eindhoven's manufacturing legacy, entry to the Philips Museum comes as part of the €18.50 Dutch Design Week entrance fee.

[9] Silvio Lorusso, looking back on the online-only Dutch Design Week in October 2020, notes that in fact: '[m]issing out is the rule.' Lorusso, S. (2021) 'Missing Out on Dutch Design Week' in *Reading Sites*. Accessed at: https://readingsites. hetnieuweinstituut.nl/missing-out-dutch-design-week-silvio-lorusso

[10] More than once I wonder about who the best people are to question or reflect on these things really are, or if there is room for organisers to critically reflect when they are responsible for the 'deliberate creation of relationship modes' themselves. It is a tricky balance. Where curators and guest countries are chosen behind closed doors, or themes that are stickered on top of a city and grown from personal curiosities, the opaque network of sponsors and capital, it is difficult to be distanced enough to be comfortable being critical.

[11] On this point, curator Katerina Gregos, in interview about the First Riga Biennial, says: 'For me it's better to have a proliferation of cultural production than to have a proliferation of football or a stupid Hollywood movie.' Barnes, F. (2018) 'Creating a Sustainable Biennial in Riga, a Look at the First RIBOCA' in *Culture Trip.* Accessed at: https://theculturetrip.com/europe/latvia/articles/creating-a-sustainable-biennial-in-riga-a-look-at-the-first-riboca/

[12] For more on this idea, see Massey, D (24 June 1991) 'A Global Sense of Place' in *Marxism Today.*

[13] In 2019, the UAE announced a new ministry — The Ministry of Possibilities — 'the world's first virtual ministry to apply design-thinking and experimentation to develop proactive and disruptive solutions to tackle critical issues, bringing together federal and local government teams and the private sector.' UAE Government (26 November 2020) 'Ministry of Possibilities'. Accessed at: https://u.ae/en/about-the-uae/the-uae-government/ministry-of-possibilities

[14] See issue #386 of *IDEA* magazine, which also cover the 29th Brno Biennial of Graphic Design. At the time, the Brno Biennial was on indefinite hiatus, in part due to its host site, the Moravian Gallery, undergoing refurbishment. The issue raised questions around what a fictional 29th Brno biennial would — or should — offer. It was later announced that the biennial will return in 2022, curated by Rick Poynor.

[15] Despite international travel being the distinction that appears between London events, it doesn't necessarily hold true for all biennials.

16 The Hostile Environment is an example of ontological design at its most horrendous. Introduced in 2012, these policies are designed so that anyone living in the UK as an undocumented migrant — ie., without a visa or 'Leave To Remain' for any reason — has their life made so administratively difficult that they might "voluntarily" choose to leave. These policies include making things like employment, renting accommodation, education, opening a bank account, and receiving healthcare impossible without full immigration paperwork. Despite these Home Office policies being widely criticised and having been found to break fundamental equality and human rights laws in a review in 2020, most remain in operation.

17 Ultimately, their position is the same, and Migrants in Culture are clear in their letter to support practitioners whilst challenging the overarching structure: 'Many freelance artists and culture workers will feel forced to participate due to their long-standing relationships with participating venues and the need to put food on the table at this time. We're not calling for the shaming of individuals and small organisations who will have to accept this money to survive. But we ask the cultural sector to join us in acknowledging and discrediting the narrative that Festival UK* 2022 is a great opportunity that should be uncritically embraced and legitimised by our involvement as artists and arts workers.'

18 A tweet, from Brendan Cormier, dated Aug 5, 2020, following catastrophic explosions in the port of Beirut: "Thinking of ways design museums, biennales and design weeks can help out Beirut. How about committing a part of one's budget this year (I know there's not a lot) to commissioning new work from Lebanese practitioners? A small way to get money flowing into the local economy." Cormier, B [@BrendanCormier] (5 August 2020) Accessed at: https:// twitter.com/BrendanCormier/ status/1290987173253132288

Bibliography

Alsaden, A. (2019) *Baghdad's Arab Biennial.* Third Text, 33(1), 121-150.

Barnes, F. (2018) *Creating a Sustainable Biennial in Riga, a Look at the First RIBOCA?* Retrieved from Culture Trip: https://theculturetrip.com/europe/latvia/articles/creating-a-sustainable-biennial-in-riga-a-look-at-the-first-riboca/

Bártolo, J. (2019, September) Editorial. *Post Millenium — Critical Essays on Contemporary Tensions: #1 Pessimism of the Intellect, Optimism of the Will* — Optimism and Foresight, pp. 7-12.

Boussard, J. (2013) London Design Festival 2012. *Design and Culture,* 5(3), pp. 410-413.

Bshara, K. (2017) *Biennales in Palestine: Thinking Art and Making Art.* PARSE(5), pp. 76-91.

Castillo, G. (2017) *Establishment Modernism and its Discontents.* In W. de Wit, *Design For the Corporate World 1950-1970,* pp. 41-60.

Connor, S. (2010) Preface. In S. Beckett, *The Unnamable* (pp. vii-xxvi). Faber & Faber.

Cormier, B. (2018, December) *Anything You Like Every Two Years. On Biennials — Where's the Party?,* 54, p. 7.

Daniels, M. (2013) *Paris National and International Exhibitions from 1798 to 1900: A Finding-List of British Library Holdings.* Retrieved from British Library: https://www.bl.uk/eblj/2013articles/pdf/ebljarticle62013.pdf

Delgado, A. (2018, May 24) *What Happened With the Havana Biennial?* Retrieved from Contemporary &: https://contemporaryand.com/magazines/what-happened-with-the-havana-biennial/

Escobar, A. (2018) *Designs for the Pluriverse.* Duke University Press.

European Commission. (n.d.). *European Capitals of Culture.* Retrieved from Culture and Creativity: https://ec.europa.eu/culture/policies/culture-cities-and-regions/european-capitals-culture

Exposure London. (2020) *The Show Must Go On.* Retrieved from https://www.facebook.com/watch/?v=726736498118711

Festival UK* 2022. (n.d.). The Vision. Retrieved from Festival UK* 2022: https://www.festival2022.uk

Fry, T. (1999) *Defuturing: A New Design Philosophy.*

Grandal Montero, G. (2012) *Biennalization? What biennalization?: the documentation of biennials and other recurrent exhibitions.* Art Libraries Journal, 37(1), 13-23.

Greenhalgh, P. (1988) *Ephemeral Vistas: The "Expositions Universelles," Great Exhibitions and World's Fairs, 1851-1939.* Manchester: Manchester University Press.

Kolb, R., & Patel, S. A. (2018, June) *Survey review and considerations.* Draft: Global Biennial Survey 2018(39), pp. 15-34.

Komorowski, W. (2018) *Hard Ground-Soft Politics: The Biennial of Graphic Arts in Ljubljana and Biting of the Iron Curtain.* Humanities, 7(97), pp. 1-16.

Koskinen, I. (2009) *Design Districts.* Design Issues, 25(4), pp. 3-12.

Lind, M. (2019) *Seven Years: The Rematerialisation of Art From 2011-2017.* Sternberg Press.

Littler, J. (2006) *Festering Britain: the 1951 Festival of Britain, decolonisation and the representation of the Commonwealth.* Visual Culture and Decolonisation in Britain, 21-42.

London Design Festival. (2020). A Note From Our Founders. Retrieved from https://londondesignfestival. com/press

Lorusso, S. (2018) *Missing Out on Dutch Design Week.* Retrieved from Reading Sites: https://readingsites. hetnieuweinstituut.nl/missing-out-dutch-design-week-silvio-lorusso

Martin, H. (2018, January 2) *How a Dutch Manufacturing Town Became a Hotbed of Design.* Retrieved from Architectural Digest: https://www. architecturaldigest.com/story/ eindhoven-dutch-manufacturing-town-design-week

Mayor of London. (2020, June 18) *Demographic breakdown of transport worker deaths from coronavirus.* Retrieved from https://www.london. gov.uk/questions/2020/1663

Merrill, L. (2015) *Most Fitting Companions: Making Mixed-Race Bodies Visible in Antebellum Public Spaces.* Theatre Survey, 56(2), pp. 138-165.

Mignolo, W. (2017, March 7) *Coloniality is Far from Over, and So Must Be Decoloniality.* Retrieved from Afterall Journal: https://www. afterall.org/publications/journal/ issue.43/coloniality-is-far-from-over-and-so-must-be-decoloniality

Mignolo, W. D. (2013, May 8) *Re:emerging, Decentring and Delinking: Shifting the Geographies of Sensing, Believing and Knowing.* Retrieved from Ibraaz: https://www. ibraaz.org/essays/59/

Mignolo, W., & Wannamaker, W. (2015) *Global Coloniality and the World Disorder: Decoloniality after Decolonization and Dewesternization after the Cold War.* Dialogue of Civilizations. World Public Forum.

Migrants in Culture. (n.d.). An Open Letter to Martin Green, the Festival UK 2022 and Oliver Dowden. Retrieved from https://docs.google. com/document/d/1r5UITmFDu4 nW4lJnqLZCAMvnFPrPaBUkN-4qMOO6_KA/edit

Migrants in Culture. (n.d.). F UK 2022. Retrieved from Migrants in Culture: http://www.migrantsinculture. com/f-uk-2022/

Nelson, C. A. (2007) *The Color of Stone: Sculpting the Black Female Subject in Nineteenth-Century America.* University Of Minnesota Press.

Neon Moire. (2021, March 1) Retrieved from https://www. instagram.com/p/CL408ncKJA4/ ?igshid=1nthiwt9uborl

Nzewi, U.-S. (2013) *The Dak'Art Biennial in the Making of Contemporary African Art, 1992-Present.* Emory University.

Pater, R. (2018) *Who Owns The City?* Retrieved from Untold Stories: http://www.untold-stories.net/?p=Who_Owns_The_City

Picard, L. (2009, October 14) *The Great Exhibition.* Retrieved from British Library: https://www.bl.uk/victorian-britain/articles/the-great-exhibition#

Szacka, L.-C. (2019) *Biennials/Triennials: Conversations on the Geography of Itinerant Display.* Columbia Books on Architecture and the City.

The Festival of Britain. (1951) *The Southbank Exhibition: A guide to the Story it Tells.*

Willis, A.-M. (2006) *Ontological Designing.* Design Philosophy Papers, 4(2), 69-92.

Youngs, I. (2020, September 9) *'Festival of Brexit' can play 'powerful role' in healing UK, organiser says.* Retrieved from BBC: https://www.bbc.co.uk/news/entertainment-arts-54069456

Colophon
Onomatopee 203.1
Design Capital 1 – The Circuit

Author
Hannah Ellis
Editors
Francisco Laranjo, Luiza Prado
and Silvio Lorusso
Published & printed by
Onomatopee
www.onomatopee.net
Design
Shared Institute

Acknowledgments
This publication was made possible
with support from: Onomatopee,
Shared Institute, and the Center for
Other Worlds.

ISBN 978-94-93148-62-8

cultuur
eindhoven